All You Can Ever Know

All You Can Ever Know

A Memoir

Nicole Chung

Catapult  New York

The author has tried to re-create events, locales, and conversations based on her own memories and those of others. In some instances, in order to maintain their anonymity, certain names, characteristics, and locations have been changed.

Copyright © 2018 by Nicole Chung
First published in the United States in 2018 by Catapult (catapult.co)
All rights reserved

ISBN: 978-1-936787-97-5

Catapult titles are distributed to the trade by Publishers Group West
Phone: 866-400-5351

Library of Congress Control Number: 2018938840

Printed in the United States of America

10 9 8 7 6 5 4 3 2 1

for Cindy

and for our daughters

. . . I wanted to know,
whoever I was, I was

—MARY OLIVER, "Dogfish"

What? You too? I thought I was the only one.

—C. S. LEWIS, *The Four Loves*

Part I

T he story my mother told me about them was always the same.

Your birth parents had just moved here from Korea. They thought they wouldn't be able to give you the life you deserved.

It's the first story I can recall, one that would shape a hundred others once I was old enough and brave enough to go looking.

When I was still young—three or four, I've been told—I would crawl into my mother's lap before asking to hear it. Her arms would have encircled me, solid and strong where I was slight, pale and freckled against my light brown skin. Sometimes, in these half-imagined memories, I picture her in the dress she wore in our only family portrait from this era, lilac with flutter sleeves—an oddly delicate choice for my solid and sensible mother. At that age, a shiny black bowl cut and bangs would have framed my face, a stark contrast to the reddish-brown perm my mother had when I was young; I was no doubt growing out of toddler cuteness by then. But my mom thought I was beautiful. When you think of someone as your gift from God, maybe you can never see them as anything else.

How could they give me up?

I must have asked her this question a hundred times, and my mother never wavered in her response. Years later I would wonder whether someone told her how to comfort me—if she read the advice in a book, or heard it from the adoption agency—or if, as my parent, she simply knew what she ought to say. What I wanted to hear.

The doctors told them you would struggle all your life. Your birth parents were very sad they couldn't keep you, but they thought adoption was the best thing for you.

Even as a child, I knew my line, too.

They were right, Mom.

By the time I was five or six years old, I had heard the tale of my loving, selfless birth parents so many times I could recite it myself. I collected every fact I could, hoarding the sparse and faded glimpses into my past like bright, favorite toys. *This may be all you can ever know*, I was told. It wasn't a joyful story through and through, but it was *their* story, and mine, too. The only thing we had ever shared. And as my adoptive parents saw it, the story could have ended no other way.

So when people asked about my family, my features, the fate I'd been dealt, maybe it isn't surprising how I answered—first in a childish, cheerful chirrup, later in the lecturing tone of one obliged to educate. I strove to be calm and direct, never giving anything away in my voice, never changing the details. Offering the story I'd learned so early was, I thought, one way to gain acceptance. It was both the excuse for how I looked, and a way of asking pardon for it.

Looking back, of course I can make out the gaps; the places where my mother and father must have made their own guesses; the pauses where harder questions could have followed: *Why didn't they ask for help? What if they had changed their minds? Would you have adopted me if you'd been able to have a child of your own?*

Family lore given to us as children has such hold over us, such staying power. It can form the bedrock of another kind of faith, one to rival any religion, informing our beliefs about ourselves, and our families, and our place in the world. When tiny, traitorous doubts arose, when I felt lost or alone or confused about all the things I couldn't know, I told myself that something as noble as my birth parents' sacrifice demanded my trust. My loyalty.

They thought adoption was the best thing for you.

Above all, it was a legend formed and told and told again because my parents wanted me to believe that my birth family had loved me from the start; that my parents, in turn, were meant to adopt me; and that the story unfolded as it should have. This was the foundation on which they built our family. As I grew, I too staked my identity on it. The story, a lifeline cast when I was too young for deeper questions, continued to bring me comfort. Years later, grown up and expecting a child of my own, I would search for my birth family still wanting to believe in it.

One afternoon in the summer of 2003, two people I had just met sat across from me in their sunny apartment and asked if I thought they should adopt. They had tried for a few years and been unable to conceive; now they wanted to adopt a child from another country. They named some programs they were interested in. None would lead to them bringing home a white child.

They asked if I ever felt like my adoptive parents weren't my "real" parents.

Never, I said firmly.

They asked if I had been in touch with my birth family.

No, I said, I hadn't.

They asked if there had ever been *any issues* when I was growing up.

I felt something like panic, the sudden shame of being found out.

Perhaps confusion was all they could read on my face, because one of them attempted to clarify: Had I ever *minded* it? Not being white, like my parents?

I wanted to answer. I liked this couple, and I knew it was my job to offer them the comfort, the encouragement they so plainly deserved. Did I *mind* not being white? It amounted to asking if I minded being Korean; *yes, I minded,* or *no, I didn't mind,* both seemed too mild for how I'd felt.

The truth was that being Korean and being adopted were things I had loved and hated in equal measure. Growing up, I was the only Korean most of my friends and family knew, the only Korean *I* knew. Sometimes the adoption—the abandonment, as I could not help but think of it when I was very young—upset me more; sometimes my differences did; but mostly, it was both at once, race and adoption, linked parts of my identity that set me apart from everyone else in my orbit. I could neither change nor deny these facts, so I worked to reconcile myself to them. To tamp down the stirring of anger or confusion when that proved impossible, time and time again.

All members of a family have their own ways of defining the others. All parents have ways of saying things about their children as if they are indisputable facts, even when the children don't believe them to be true at all. It's why so many of us sometimes feel alone or unseen, despite the real love we have for our families and they for us. In childhood, I was uncertain who I was supposed to be, even as I resisted some of my adoptive relatives' interpretations—both *you're our Asian Princess!* and *of course we don't* think *of you as Asian.* I believe my adoptive family, for the most part, wanted to ignore the fact that I was the product of people from the other side of the world, unknown foreigners turned Americans. To them, I was not the daughter of these immigrants at all: by adopting me, my parents had made me one of them.

And perhaps I never would have felt differently—perhaps I, too, would have thought of myself as *almost* white—but for all the people who never indulged this fantasy beyond my home, my family, the reach of my parents' eyes. Caught between my family's "colorblind" ideal and the obvious notice of others, perhaps it isn't surprising which made me feel safer—which I preferred, and tried to adopt as my own.

Somewhere along the way, though, after leaving home, I had

learned to feel strangely proud of my heritage. I'd made friends in middle school and high school who liked and accepted me even though I was one of the few Asian kids they knew. Then I had gone off to college and found myself living among huge numbers of fellow Asians; on campus, which soon felt more like home than the town where I had lived all my life, I finally learned how it felt to exist in a space, walk into a classroom, and not be stared at. I loved being just one Asian girl among thousands. Every day, I felt relieved to have found a life where I was no longer surrounded by white people who had no idea what to make of me.

Still, I did not know what it meant to be a Korean completely sundered from her culture, or if I could truly call myself a Korean at all—when my Korean American dormmate in college referred to me as a "banana," I knew enough to understand it was not a compliment, but had no real defense. To me Korea was little more than a faraway country, less real to me than a fantasy, and my own Korean family existed in an alternate timeline I could hardly begin to imagine. I had yet to grapple with or resolve my adoption's place in my life, what it meant and how I ought to think of it—at twenty-two, sitting in my new friends' dining room, a genuine, perhaps more generous understanding of who I was still flickered beyond my reach.

I looked from one pair of earnest eyes to the other, wondering how I could explain all this to them. How had I gotten here? How had I become the voice of reassurance for two people about to embark on parenthood? I'd been out of college a matter of weeks. I still had trouble thinking of myself as an adult. I had no idea what it took to raise a child, let alone one whose face would announce to everyone that they weren't born into their family.

My hometown is a five-hour drive from Portland, nestled in a valley in sight of three mountain ranges. For years now, when I go home, it has been my ritual to step off the plane and begin counting the people of color in the town's one-room airport; often, there's only me. I spent eighteen years there without getting to know another Korean.

Once my parents and I left our little house on Alma Drive, we were bound to turn heads. *Where did they get you?* people at the grocery store asked. Or, on the playground, *How much did you cost?* Kids at school wanted to know why I didn't look like them. Teachers stumbled over my Hungarian surname, looking perplexed even after my corrections.

To my family's credit, my adoption was never kept secret from me—not that it could have been, I suppose. I avoided the fate of adopted children of earlier generations, who were often told about their adoptions late in adolescence, as adults, or not at all. An adopted woman I met once told me she didn't learn she was adopted until she was a teenager, an echo of other stories I'd heard before. She found out by accident; friends and relatives knew, and one day someone let slip the neighborhood secret.

My parents explained my adoption when I was too young to remember, adding details over the years until I knew almost everything they did. Just as I don't remember the day I learned I was adopted, I don't remember precisely when I realized I was practically the only Asian I ever saw—but I imagine it must have been sometime in kindergarten, my first year of school. I was already aware that no one in my family looked like me—nor did anyone in our neighborhood, or in my grandmother's neighborhood across town—but it hadn't mattered much in the years before I stepped through the doors of our town's only Catholic school, because I knew so little about people beyond the circle of my own family.

There were around twenty-five kids in my afternoon kindergarten class, every one of them white. At morning circle, on the playground, packed into the pews during school-wide Masses, at assemblies and concerts and sporting events, it was the same: white child after white parent, face after face that looked nothing like mine. By the age of five, I must have had words like *Korean* and *Asian* to describe myself, because I remember deploying such terms at school. I might have also possessed a vague, sight-based under-standing of whiteness. But having never talked about race with any-one before, I couldn't have strung together the words to describe what I was seeing—or not seeing—just as I couldn't have told any-one why it suddenly mattered.

And at first, in truth, it wasn't *so* difficult to be the only Asian girl in my class. A particularly innocent classmate once asked me, "Are you black?" and this was easily answered. One of so many towheaded girls said, "Mary did *not* have black hair!" when the Christmas pageant rolled around, and I decided that was fine, be-cause the angels got wings and better songs. I knew I was different, but during kindergarten I believed it was simply a fact, one that caused me little distress.

In first grade, when I took my turn as the designated "Very Important Person," I brought in my family photos glued to white poster board as all the kids before me had. My classmates, arranged in a semicircle on the woven rug, naturally wanted to know why all of my pictures showed me flanked by my redheaded, freckled white mom and early-graying white dad, though that wasn't what they said—what they said was, "Are those your parents? How come you don't look like them?" I spent most of my presentation explaining matters, but I didn't mind much; it was thrilling, in a way, to hold so many of my classmates in thrall. A strange feeling spiked, the earliest suspicion that I might eventually spend a great deal of time answering people's questions about adoption, but I told myself it was fine. How lucky that I already knew so much about it.

Then one of my classmates thrust his hand in the air. His face was expectant—and a little reproachful, as though I'd stopped read-ing just before the end of a rollicking good story and was deliber-ately keeping everyone in suspense. "Don't you want to meet your *real* parents?"

No one in my family ever referred to my birth parents as my real parents. But once I got over my initial shock, I understood why he had asked. Of course the other kids would be curious about my birth family. Of course they would want to solve the mystery I, too, obsessed over.

In the years to come I would hear variations on this same question, over and over, and it would never again surprise me—I just never knew what to say. What did it matter what I *wanted*? I *wasn't* going to meet them.

When it was time to gather up my poster and return to my seat, I was glad I'd had the opportunity to tell my story. I could still tell myself that the unknown or confusing aspects of my history didn't matter; that none of my classmates really cared that I was Korean, or that my family wasn't like theirs. It was the last year I would be able to pretend that was true.

Facing the hopeful couple across from me, I knew I had to speak. We had been introduced by mutual friends precisely so I could tell them how wonderful it was to grow up adopted. "I just think it would be great for them to talk to you," my friend had told me when she set up the meeting. I was there—I had agreed to go!—to offer reassuring statements about being raised by white parents who loved me. I *wanted* to be helpful. Why was I hesitating?

Ten, even five years earlier, it would have posed no great challenge; I'd never shied away from the story I grew up hearing. By the time a friend in middle school asked me what it was like to be adopted—as if I could compare it to anything else—I knew just how to laugh, just what to say. *Most people are stuck with their kids*, I told her, rather insufferably. *My parents* chose *me*. But I was out of practice, having spent the past four years at a university whose enrollment was one-quarter Asian. Friends and classmates and professors who had never seen me with my parents had little reason to ask if I was adopted. And when I did mention it now, when I told people like my college roommate or my faculty advisor or even my boyfriend, Dan, the fact emerged as a biographical footnote: people usually nodded and filed the information away, even if I did sometimes see curiosity spark in their eyes. My two worlds were three thousand miles and a world of experience apart, and rarely collided.

When Dan met my parents, in October of my junior year, I was so anxious—I remember being irrationally convinced that he wouldn't be able to understand or find common ground with them, generous and kind as he was. When he asked me why, I could only come up with one answer: *We're just so different.* The old self-consciousness, the archetypically adolescent *God, you guys are so embarrassing* familiar to any teenager, had given way to the less cringing but still sure knowledge that my parents and I were opposites in every conceivable way, from how we looked to the ways our minds worked. They tended to act less like my parents and more like my peers; they were always telling me I worked too much, thought too much, *cared* too much. *We weren't really prepared to have a kid like you,* my mother had said once, something she might have regretted if she were in the habit of questioning her words.

Even without this revelation, though, I would have known. I had always felt like the much-adored but still obvious alien in the family. I knew we didn't always make sense to other people. And of course my adoption, the obvious explanation for it, was right there, but I could never bring myself to reference it—not even to Dan. It felt petty and wrong, like I was assigning blame to something I was supposed to be grateful for. I still wanted our family to pass muster as "normal," whatever that meant, and so our differences—and how I came to belong to my parents—were not supposed to matter. Not to anyone we met, and certainly not to me.

Now, facing *Did you mind it?* from people I liked, people who wanted to become parents just like mine had, I was not yet thinking of their future child; I wanted to reassure *them.* I could see compassion and silent encouragement in their eyes, the promise of friendship, a churning worry they couldn't entirely hide. Something about them tripped every quiet doubt, every fiercely protective instinct I'd ever had about my own family. Here were two potential parents who were ready to believe in adoption and so, by extension, the goodness and rightness of my own upbringing. How could I explain what it had been like? How my presence in my family, and especially in the town where I grew up, had often made so little sense to me? How could I tell them that their child might feel the same way, no matter how much they were loved?

These people weren't my parents. I knew that. But they seemed *meant* to be parents, if anyone was, and I could already tell they had the best of intentions. They wanted a child badly enough to open up to a near-stranger, make themselves vulnerable and lay their fears bare. Their longing for a baby to love, for things to work out in their favor, couldn't help but move me.

Though I felt like I'd been stalling, considering their question for far too long, it was probably only the space of a few breaths. I stretched my mouth into a smile. I tried to radiate the real warmth I felt toward them, though we had only just met. I leaned forward a little in my chair, and I told them no. No, there were no big "issues." I'd been loved. I'd been okay. Their child would be okay, too.

I was rewarded with twin beams of happiness and relief, and I found myself smiling wider in spite of myself. I could tell they weren't especially surprised. Of course I had been okay. I was sitting here now, with them, wasn't I—healthy, happy, well-adjusted, weeks away from a bachelor's degree, an engagement ring on my finger? Clearly everything in my life had worked out fine. Their child would be just fine, too. That was what they had wanted, expected to hear, all along.

I was in second or third grade when I heard my first slur.

I argued with a boy on the playground—I don't remember the reason. He called me *ugly*, which stung a bit, but it was also the sort of generic insult kids flung at one another all the time. If he'd stopped there, it might have remained a remote, laughable memory, a childhood squabble buried alongside dozens of other such moments.

Instead, he pulled his eyes into slits. His voice turned shrill as he sneered, "You're so ugly, your own parents didn't even want you!"

It was the first time anyone had ever used my adoption as an insult, and it would have been shocking and painful enough without the eyes, the broken singsong chant. He screwed up his face into a squint, asking how I could see. "Me Chinee, me can't see!"

Was "Chinee" supposed to be a nickname? I did not know what it meant, but I instinctively understood that he wasn't making fun of something about me, or something I had done. He wasn't mocking a name I could change into a nickname, or clothes my parents could replace, or glasses I could take off at recess. His target was who I *was*. How I'd come to be here, in this place where he believed I did not belong.

I waited, almost in suspense, for my own voice to emerge, for my sharp tongue to go on the attack. But any return insults withered and died in my throat. I couldn't have been more passive had I been invisible, a ghost floating high above the blacktop, watching the other kids laughing and feeling surprised, just as any witness or casual observer might, by my own shame and silence.

He made more faces, his eyes still pulled back tight; I wondered if *he* could see. To anyone watching, I probably looked eerily calm— the same girl I'd always been. This boy was in my carpool, and lived in my neighborhood, and until this day I'd thought of him as a kind of friend. When we rode home together that afternoon, side by side in the backseat of his mother's blue sedan, I was silent and so was he, pretending nothing had happened between us that day. But inside of me, something still and deep, something precious, had broken.

After that day, when I heard more words like that from him and other classmates—when adults I met questioned my nationality or my lack of an accent, or measured me against Asian stereotypes that were true in their minds—I would, to some degree, *expect* it. Each and every time I found myself on the defensive, defining an identity that seemed to require endless explanations, it would remind me of that day at recess when I learned what a slur *meant*, even if I did not yet know the name for it. And maybe I should have known to be angry as a child. Maybe I should have realized that others were the problem, not me. But hadn't I already been suspicious before that day when my neighbor's words hit the bull's-eye? Hadn't I already wondered if *I* might be wrong, taking up space where I did not have a right to? The self-consciousness I'd felt but hardly known how to track since starting at that small white school bloomed to sudden, painful awareness. If I wasn't safe with a boy who'd known me for years, who knew where I lived, whose mother knew mine, then I couldn't trust anyone.

I remember I could tell my parents only part of the truth. I said that someone had made fun of me for being adopted. I didn't mention the other words the boy had used. This felt like a different kind of humiliation, one I could not expect them to understand. They had always insisted the fact that I was Korean didn't matter; what mattered was "the kind of person" I was. How could I tell them they were wrong?

If my parents were surprised or upset, they didn't show it. They have both always possessed a rather low opinion of human nature, and spitefulness, even outright cruelty, from an ignorant boy could not have shocked them. My mother said that he shouldn't have teased me for being adopted. "He's only doing it to get a reaction," she told me.

"If you ignore him, he'll stop," my father agreed.

I tried, but the schoolyard taunts multiplied, spreading beyond the first boy to other classmates. When they tried out new words, or told me to go back to China, or babbled in their made-up languages, no one stood up for me. Kids I'd known since kindergarten now seemed like strangers—either hostile, or else somehow remote and inaccessible. I had not changed, and maybe they hadn't, either, but when they looked at me it was as if we'd never known each other at all.

At our school, you were with the same kids grade after grade, the same boys with saints' names and the same pretty, fair-haired girls. Who you were in second grade was who you were in fourth grade and who you were in sixth. So the taunts continued, all the way until I completed sixth grade and moved on to another school, where sometimes I still heard the same words. Remembering my parents' advice, I tried not to react to the pulled-back eyes, the stinging chants, the cold shoulder from kids I'd once thought of as friends. The closest anyone ever got to noticing what was going on was when my second-grade teacher alluded to my general unhappiness on my third-quarter report card. But my grades were always good, and I was targeted only when there were no teachers around. If I was isolating myself more and more at school, retreating to the library as often as possible, well, I'd always been a bookish child.

I never had a name for what was happening. I had never heard or read about any racism other than the kind that outright destroys your life and blots out your physical existence; even that was relegated in books and lessons to "it happened in the past." What I experienced on the elementary school playground, and then later on my middle school bus, and for the rest of my years in southern Oregon when people demanded to know where I was from and why I had a white family, always seemed too insignificant to be even remotely connected to *real* racism. My parents and I had certainly never discussed the possibility that I might encounter bigots within my school, our neighborhood, our family, in places they believed were safe for me.

The strange thing was that, inside, I always felt I *was* the same as everyone around me. *I am just like you,* I thought when kids squinted at me in mockery of my own eyes; *why can't you see that?* When I was young I certainly felt more like a white girl than an Asian one, and sometimes it was shocking to catch a glimpse of my face in the mirror and be forced to catalog the hated differences; to encounter tormentors and former friends and know that what they saw was so at odds with the person I believed I was. Why did I have to look the way I did—like a foreigner; like my birth parents, two people I would never even meet? Why hadn't my adoption transformed me into the person I felt I was?

If I were a heroine in a fairy tale, I often thought, and a fairy godmother offered to grant me wishes, I would ask for peaches-and-cream skin, eyes like deep blue pools, hair like spun gold instead of blackest ink. I knew I would be worthy of it all. There was nothing I wouldn't trade for that kind of magic, that kind of beauty. If you were pretty, if you were normal, if you were *white*, then the good things everyone saw on the outside would match the goodness you knew existed on the inside. And wouldn't it be wonderful to go to sleep one night and wake up an entirely different person, one who would be loved and welcomed everywhere? Wouldn't it be wonderful to look at your face in the mirror and know you would always belong?

When the couple hoping to adopt asked me what it had been like to grow up the Korean child of white parents—Was it *all right*? Had I ever *minded* it?—I didn't want to tell them that I had minded not being white every day for years on end. That sometimes it still bothered me, because while I had finally found another life for myself, my story was still not quite what others expected when they saw me.

And I didn't want to tell them about the day my parents and teachers finally caught me twirling my hair, the black hair that was so unlike the beautiful blond hair I wanted, twisting it around and around the first joint of my forefinger so tightly I couldn't free it without yanking a few strands out. After my alarmed parents spotted the tiny bald spot on the left side of my head, I spent a year and a half in play therapy with a counselor named Charlotte. Once a week, I followed her into her expansive office/playroom, tucked up in the gable of a stately old house, where we played dress-up and painted pictures of our fears. I talked to Charlotte about how I felt, though now I cannot remember what I said; I know she in turn talked to my parents.

An Asian baby doll appeared under the tree one Christmas, specially ordered, though I was probably a little too old for dolls. At nine, I turned on the television one night to discover Kristi Yamaguchi, my first Asian American childhood hero, being cheered by crowds and adored in a way I did not think people who looked like me could be. I wrote stories, dozens of them, about other people, other lives I craved. I stopped twirling my hair. Eventually, I stopped seeing the therapist. But I would never forget the hair-pulling, would never be able to think of it without deep and terrible shame. If I still felt I did not belong, I decided I could not allow others to see it. The only way out of my school, out of this town, was to grow up and leave—I could not wallow in fear or sadness again if I wanted to escape.

And escape I did: by the time I met the young wife and husband who were nothing and everything like my own parents, I had run as far as I could to college and spent years fighting to define myself in ways that had nothing to do with being Korean or adopted. The old "race-blind" view of my adoption was one I was just beginning to question in my early twenties. Now I was able to call out bigotry only when it was staring me in the face, and never without a deeply self-conscious blush, a pounding heart, and sharp, squirming discomfort.

Unbidden, a memory surfaced: a day in fourth or fifth grade when a group of white girls had climbed up close to my perch on the monkey bars. I'd felt such hope when I saw their smiles. Had they changed their minds about me? One of them, whose particular shade of blond hair was ashier, whose face was sharper and not as pretty as some of the others', leaned toward me, her voice low: "We have a question, Nicole, and you're the only one we can ask." And though I had been conditioned, through years of experience, to expect a trap, still I was momentarily taken in, expecting a friendly word or an invitation to play—until she said in a louder voice, "Do you have a sideways vagina? My brother told me Asian girls have those."

And I knew this and other such moments from my childhood were almost laughably tame compared to what other people of color endured. Was it my place to explain as much to this hopeful couple? To warn them that even if their adopted child's race didn't matter to *them*, it would matter to others—that it would be brought up, in countless situations they could not hope to control, in ways and in words that might not even reach their ears? Before I could decide, one of them asked the question I had known was coming.

"Do *you* think we should adopt?"

They had already investigated and ranked international adoption programs. They had discussed their favorite baby names. The room still smelled like the delicious meal the wife had cooked for us, and their comfortable apartment felt so much more like a home than my own tiny place, still filled with secondhand furniture and posters I'd bought in college. These people were only four or five years older than me, but they were *adults*—responsible, settled, employed, and not just eager but ready to be parents. They both came from loving, supportive families excited to welcome their children through birth, or adoption, or both. I couldn't bring myself to say anything that would make them reconsider the goodness of their plans, or the rightness of families that looked like mine.

My brain, or maybe my fiercely loyal adoptee heart, scrambled and rewrote the question I'd been set. *Did I think they would love their child?* Of course. And they would do their best. What more could they do? What more could *anyone* do?

"Absolutely," I heard myself say. "Adoption is no big deal. It's just another way to join a family. I know I was very lucky, and your child will be, too."

It's not that I think I gave the wrong answer, or that there was a right or wrong answer to begin with. Today, when I'm asked, I often say that I no longer consider adoption—individual adoptions, or adoption as a practice—in terms of *right* or *wrong*. I urge people to go into it with their eyes open, recognizing how complex it truly is; I encourage adopted people to tell their stories, our stories, and let no one else define these experiences for us.

But back then, I still had to think of adoption as an unqualified good, a benefit to every adoptee, sure proof of unselfish love, because to do otherwise felt like a betrayal of my family and their love for me. I still remember how good it felt, how *right*, to reassure that couple in the moment. I did not have to tell them any of the things I was so ashamed to remember. I did not have to burden them with knowledge of all the ways I had never quite fit in. Their future child wasn't me; their family was not mine. They just wanted to be happy, and why shouldn't they be?

The wife gave me a long hug at the door. "I hope our kid grows up to be *just* like you," she said. As I left, I was aware of no internal second guesses, no prickings of conscience. What I said to them wasn't a lie, I thought, nor was it cowardice or denial. I *was* lucky. I *was* grateful. What would have happened to me if I had never been adopted? These people were trying to write their own story, build a beautiful family against the odds. I was glad I wouldn't walk away from them wondering if I'd broken it up before it had even begun. I was glad they wouldn't remember me as the person who'd made them question their happy ending.

M y parents' story together began in the spring of 1973 when they married and struck out west. She was twenty-one, he was twenty-two, and they'd been dating a matter of months when she told him she was leaving Cleveland, a city she had never much liked, for Seattle—where she had always planned to live, and where her own mother had spent the war years, living with her aunt and her uncle, the Swedish fisherman. My mother had not inherited much from her mother, save her red hair, quick temper, and stubborn attachment to the green beauty of provincial Washington State, so different from the smoke and cement of Cleveland and the small farm community outside it where her family lived. She had been to Seattle, carted along on cross-country road trips in the family station wagon, to visit her great-aunt and great-uncle, and she'd never forgotten the pine-scented air or the snow-tipped mountains wreathed in clouds, the hilly city lapped at its edges by a cold saltwater sound. Now she had gotten into nursing school out there—so, was he coming with her or not?

Though their families charged them with desertion, the move had its appeal: they were each one of five siblings, high in the birth order, and in different but defining ways their parents had been hard on them. More than three hundred people attended their wedding. Back then, it was still a little unusual for a Hungarian boy from one neighborhood to marry a Polish girl from another. There were fist-icuffs at the reception, and it was generally agreed that the bride's relatives both began and ended the fight, but everyone was laughing by the time they farewelled the couple.

They did move out west, but not to Seattle; not yet. A printing company had offered him a job in Ketchikan, Alaska, on Revilla-gigedo Island in the Alexander Archipelago. She found a job at the local hospital. They rented a basement apartment in a cottage on the edge of the Inside Passage, where they could step outside and watch eagles wheeling over the ruffled water. For a pair of born-and-bred Clevelanders, Ketchikan was almost too quaint to be believed with its fishermen and modest tourist trade, its streets and wooden pil-ings slick with rain one hundred and forty days out of the year. It was not quite the change she had envisioned, but a chance it still was, to escape Ohio and try on a different life. They liked it there, and felt like pioneers.

Still, when the transfer to Seattle came a few years later, they were ready to live in a city again, eager to meet new people. One Sunday, on a whim, they visited a little white-steepled church set into the hills above the neighborhood where they rented an attic apartment. It was nothing like the large, drafty old churches they'd attended as children in Cleveland; everyone wore jeans. The priest's gentle Polish accent reminded her of her beloved grandfather, but it was someone else at the parish who commandeered their attention: a short, stout nun with blunt brown bangs peeking out from under her minimal wimple, a far cry from the strict, ruler-wielding sisters of their youth. They told Sister Mary Francis they had little interest in organized religion, let alone the church in which they'd both been raised, but the nun somehow convinced them to return. Soon my mother was leading a Bible-study group and my father was running errands for Sister Mary Francis's elderly mother. They were back in the fold, with barely a token argument raised in their own defense.

This time, though, they were changed: they believed it all. They asked God to move in their lives. They saw his hand at work—in friends met, in jobs found, in day-to-day life—where they had never looked for him before.

It was through their new parish that they met Liz: a woman of towering faith, another smile in a sea of friendly faces, but no one they thought would change their lives. Years later, in the summer of 1981, after he had been transferred, one last time, to southern Oregon; after nearly a decade of marriage, half of it spent hoping for children that never came; after they had finally started looking into adoption as a last resort, Liz was the one who called to tell them about a premature baby at the Seattle Children's Hospital, a girl who'd beaten the odds. A baby girl who needed a family.

They had always planned to have children, though they hadn't been in a hurry. Kids had always come along in their big Catholic families, sometimes in pairs, often by surprise. But she got pregnant only once and had been carrying a matter of weeks when they found out the fetus had no heartbeat.

They were told that couples facing infertility should grieve the loss of biological children, the hopes raised and disappointed cycle after cycle, before they moved forward with adoption. For them, though, spending years or even months in mourning didn't feel right. The miscarriage had been devastating, but they had already resigned themselves to the fact that biological children might not be in their future. If adoption was God's plan for them, she said, she didn't mind missing out on the experiences of pregnancy and birth. She joked, when she was ready to joke about it, that if someone else did all that work instead, it would be okay with her. They both just wanted a baby. If they were lucky enough to be able to adopt, they would never dwell on things they had been denied.

When Liz called to tell them about the baby in Seattle, it felt as if God was finally smiling down on them. And when their friend added, almost as an afterthought, that the baby was Korean, it could not temper their enthusiasm. They might have to warn their families, particularly their parents. But they had been hoping and praying for a child to adopt, and what was Liz's call if not the Lord choosing to answer their prayers? What did the child's color matter, in the end, when they had so much love to give? It would be unseemly, ungrateful to focus on a thing like race in the face of such a gift. *It wouldn't have mattered to us if you were black, white, or purple with polka dots*, they would tell their daughter over and over, once she was old enough to understand the story of how she came to them.

Odd as that declaration would sound to me, every time, I would always believe them.

Liz's mother worked in a doctor's office, and one of the practitioners had been approached by a colleague, a pediatrician, who asked if he knew of anyone who might be interested in adopting a baby. Liz heard the news from her mother, then went home and prayed before calling her friends in Oregon. She knew they wanted to adopt and had just completed a home study through a Catholic Charities adoption program. The doctor told Liz's mother that if a couple hired an attorney as opposed to going through an adoption agency, things might move faster.

With Liz's help, they found a family law attorney in Seattle named Kathy. She agreed to represent them—if they were sure they wanted to proceed with "the Korean child." Were they? If they were honest with themselves, the child's rocky start in life was far more worrisome than her ethnicity. They had only just begun the adoption process and had not yet compiled a list of what might be, for them, disqualifying circumstances. They had never made much money. Could they take care of a child who might never live independently? What if she needed round-the-clock care?

So she put a fleece before the Lord. It was an act of faith, a test of what she could not see, but it was also informed by her years of working in hospitals, seeing premature infants in the NICU. The ones who tended to struggle most were the ones who had spent weeks on a ventilator. She told God that if the baby had never been kept alive with the aid of a machine, then she would take it as a sign that it was all right to proceed.

They prayed for guidance. They prayed for God's will to be done. They knew they could wait, of course, for a child in better health, but it was so much harder to say no to a real possibility. A real baby.

A week later, Liz connected them with a pediatrician at the hospital, who shared the baby's brief history. She had been born approximately ten weeks short of full term. She still had no hair, just the suggestion of future eyebrows. She was a favorite of the nurses and had been steadily gaining weight, ounce by hard-won ounce. There was no way to predict what her future might hold. But, Liz had been told, the girl had never relied on a ventilator. She came out breathing on her own.

It was the sign they had been waiting for; the sign they needed. They were meant to be this little girl's parents.

Kathy hadn't facilitated many adoptions—she would handle only ten or so over the course of her legal career. By coincidence, she had her own slight connection to the birth parents: she had been to the store they owned. Years later, during a chance meeting at that same store, the baby's mother would recognize Kathy and ask what had happened to her child; if the hopeful adoptive parents had known this would happen, perhaps they would have chosen another lawyer.

Now that they had a real child in their sights, they wanted to move quickly. They didn't ask many questions about their would-be daughter's family, even though Kathy knew them. They didn't want to meet the couple or learn their names. Even talking about them felt like a risk. Their family-to-be, the one they could finally see in their minds, was still little more than a wish—the all-too-fragile arrangement might fall apart if they pushed too hard in any one place.

So there was never any prolonged discussion about the birth family's social history, nor was there any discussion about a more open adoption, which would have been highly uncommon at the time. Surely what any child of any color or background needed, most of all, was *stability*. They had to establish their own relationship with the girl, free from outside interference or fear of legal challenge.

The birth parents didn't have their own legal representation—perhaps they couldn't afford it, or perhaps they thought it unnecessary. Kathy talked with them a couple of times, mostly to pass along the adoptive parents' wishes and make sure all the paperwork was in order. She believed the child's birth father had been the one to initiate the adoption; the birth mother, she thought, seemed less certain. But both parents agreed and both parents signed, and anyway, they weren't Kathy's clients.

All parties agreed to a closed adoption, with no information exchanged and no further contact planned. *Boilerplate*, the lawyer would later call it. With no outlandish requests on either side, paperwork moved along at an impressive clip. Officially it was deemed a "special-needs adoption," and no one wanted to force a vulnerable child to spend weeks or months in temporary care. By law, the placement could not be finalized for a full six months, but the adoptive parents could get custody upon the child's release from the hospital.

When they told their families of their plans, no one tried to talk them out of adopting a Korean baby. Their parents and siblings all knew how much they wanted to be parents. Probably no one dreamed that anyone in the family might harbor opinions or prejudices that would compromise their ability to love the girl. No matter what you might think about Asian people (*weird food   anchor babies   inscrutable robots   good at math*), it's different when it's *your* Asian daughter or cousin, granddaughter or niece, isn't it? Many years later, the parents and grandmother would laugh over how one of her cousins managed to reach the age of twelve without realizing the girl wasn't born into their family. As far as most of the relatives were concerned, the adoption might as well have leached the melanin from the child's skin and hair, rounded the corners of her eyes, erased her family tree entirely. Those papers made her one of them, no matter where—or whom—she'd come from.

Three weeks after learning about the child, they drove up to Seattle. Before they could go to the hospital and get their baby, they had to sit through an interview with a King County social worker. Like Kathy before her, the social worker had spoken to the child's parents and was convinced they really did want to release her for adoption. "I don't understand it," she said, with a frankness that surprised the parents a little. "I tried and tried to talk them out of it."

The social worker didn't call the birth parents by their names, first or last, when referring to them—"The family name is unpronounceable!" she insisted—and made no effort to hide how confused she was. The birth parents were married; they had a stable, if not enormously profitable family business; they had children at home who had reportedly been looking forward to having a little sister. They'd been shocked by the baby's premature arrival, true, and like many immigrants and small business owners, they did not carry health insurance. They seemed to believe the doctors' direst predictions and thought they couldn't provide a good home for the child. As best as she could with no Korean, no translator, and the birth parents' self-conscious English—good on the father's part, in particular, but lacking in legal vocabulary—the social worker had given the birth parents a lengthy explanation of their rights and every opportunity to change their minds. When she tried to tell them about available resources and assistance, they just shook their heads.

"If the birth parents ever try to challenge the adoption or regain custody, I'll speak for you," the social worker said. They twitched, nervous at the mere suggestion. "I told them they didn't have to do this."

The birth parents had asked if the new parents could cover some of the girl's medical bills. The requested portion amounted to less than three thousand dollars. Compared to most infant adoptions, it was a real bargain. Eventually, the adoptive mother asked about the child's race: Was there anything they ought to know, given that she was Korean? Was there anything special they should do for her?

The social worker seemed surprised by the question. She looked at them for a moment, then shook her head. "I'm sure you'll all be fine."

They tore their baby out of the arms of a hospital nurse on July 21, then packed her into the car and headed south on I-5. They stopped three times along the way to help her down a bottle of formula, arriving back at their snug ranch house in the cul-de-sac nine hours later.

They thought their daughter was just beautiful, with her dark, dark eyes and bump of a nose. She still had no eyelashes or eyebrows and very little hair on her head. But she already had the chubbiest cheeks. *Buddha baby*, they called her, laughing. She weighed less than six pounds—still barely newborn-size, at two and a half months old—and fit entirely in one of her father's hands. She was alert and very serious, but learning how to smile.

She was also noisier than they had expected. She talked and talked and talked, her tone rising and falling in babbles and gurgles that sounded almost conversational. She lasted three days in their room, happily chattering at intervals through the night, before they had to move her crib to another room so they could get some sleep.

Sometimes they could still hear her from her room across the hall, conversing with unseen friends in her own made-up language. Her mother would groan a little, regret over lost sleep being one of the first rites of initiation for any new parent. Her father would joke, "She's talking to her angels again."

No matter how a child joins your family, their presence changes all the rules; they move into your heart and build new rooms, knock down walls you never knew existed. This is why new parents crave reassurance more than anything else: We tell ourselves, and want others to tell us, that we're going to be wonderful parents. That our children will be happy. That their suffering will be light—or at least, never of a kind we cannot help them through. We have to believe these things, promise ourselves we'll meet every challenge, or we'd never be brave enough to begin.

No one ever so much as hinted to my parents that adopting across racial and cultural lines might prove a unique challenge, one they needed to prepare for specifically. If they did take a "color-blind" view of our family from its very formation—if they believed my Koreanness was irrelevant within our family, and should be so to everyone else as well—in this they were largely following ideals they were raised with, advice they had been given. Often, when I meet fellow transracial adoptees, we find we can share like experiences: *My parents and I almost never talked about race. We didn't really acknowledge that it mattered. I never called anyone in my family out about their racism.* Even now, when there is more awareness, more "celebration" of adopted children's cultures, many parents are not provided with the guidance or resources they need to bring up children of color in white families, white communities, a white supremacist society. To fault only my white parents for not fully understanding the things they were shielded from—first by professionals and later by me—is to miss the larger point: we were and are representative of so many transracial and transcultural adoptions from that era.

So many times I have tried to imagine that winter day in the King County courthouse—the day my adoption was finalized—a half year after my parents took me from the nursery of the Seattle Children's Hospital. I picture some middle-aged, balding judge peering down from the bench at my father, still dark-haired with no traces of gray, looking serious for once in his life; my mother with her creamy freckled skin and nervous smile, cradling me in a pink blanket monogrammed with my new name in a flowing script. My parents had spent the past six months learning how to care for me, trying not to heed any lingering fears about my birth parents reversing their decision. Like many new parents, they hoped to do the best they could and expected that would always be sufficient.

I'm told the judge spoke very seriously with them about their decision, the commitment they had made to me and to the state. There was no changing their minds now: they were my real parents, my only parents, under the law. Thrilled to affix an official state seal to what they already knew in their hearts, my parents asked the judge if he had any advice.

I wonder if he was surprised by their question, as the social worker had been, or if it was one he expected, one he'd even heard countless times from white parents of brown and black children. Did he perhaps respond without thinking, already informed by years of experience? Did he offer all such families the same advice? Or did he look closely at my young, eager parents and consider them, specifically, before answering?

"Just assimilate her into your family," he said, "and everything will be fine. She's yours now."

She's yours. These were the words my parents had hoped to hear ever since they made the decision, years ago, to have a child. They thanked the judge, smiling as they accepted his congratulations. Then they bundled me up against the January chill, walked out of the courthouse, and brought me home.

Cindy would never be able to recall anyone actually telling her the baby had died.

She was six years old, too young to know where babies came from, but for months she had known her mother had one in her belly. No one sat her down to explain it; there was no chipper announcement, no family meeting or meal at which she was told, *You're going to be a big sister soon.* She rarely had long conversations with either of her parents. They were always stressed over money and the small business they owned, the store where Cindy also spent most of her waking hours.

When Cindy was a baby, her parents had moved to America with her half sister, Jessica. Jessica was almost twelve, old enough to be helpful as they worked to establish the family business. Cindy stayed behind with her father's mother in Korea; later, she lived with other relatives in Hawaii. She did not rejoin her parents until she was five years old. And so, at six, she was still getting to know her mother and father. She knew they were strict. She knew they often argued. She knew they worked from sunup to long after dark, always on their feet.

Cindy learned to work hard, too, to keep her head down, keep quiet, do as she was told. Before school, she helped at the store, unloading inventory, stocking the shelves, sweeping the floors, chasing dirt and dust bunnies away with a feather duster. After school, she did the same, often remaining there with her parents and sister until midnight. Her world was very small: home, the store, her school, the store again. No days off, no vacations. *What kind of a family is this?* Jessica would sometimes grouse, but it was all Cindy knew and she hadn't yet begun to question it.

Years later, she would wonder how she even knew about her mother's pregnancy. Maybe Jessica told her? Or maybe she heard the news from their grandmother, their mother's mother, who lived with them for a time? However she found out, she knew there would be much more to do with a new baby to take care of. Cindy hoped she could help. She tried to picture the baby sleeping at the store while the rest of them worked.

Her mother was a small woman to begin with, and her belly, even when she was several months pregnant, was only slightly rounded. You wouldn't have known she was expecting just by looking at her. Later Cindy learned that her mother bound her stomach tightly each morning before she went to work. Cindy did not ask, but every day she wondered how much longer they would have to wait for the baby to be born.

One day that spring Cindy's mother erupted, yelling at her over something—Cindy would never remember what she had done to provoke her. Perhaps she hadn't done anything at all. As she always did, even when she knew it was unfair, Cindy lowered her eyes and held her tongue while her mother shouted. Talking back only made things worse.

When she looked up, her mother was leaning over a chair, face twisted in pain. She wasn't shouting anymore. Something was wrong. Her grandmother ran and fetched hot cloths to lay on her mother's stomach, but it didn't seem to help. Her mother squeezed her eyes shut. She panted and paced, and sometimes she cried out.

The baby is coming, Cindy heard her say.

Her mother's belly was too small. The baby wasn't supposed to be born yet. Despite her pain and fear, her mother did not want to go to the hospital: hospitals and doctors cost money. But finally, when it became clear the baby wasn't going to wait, she agreed to go.

At home, Cindy waited. She had always been very good at waiting.

When her parents came home without a baby, she and Jessica didn't know what to think. And then, eventually, Cindy found out the baby had died in the hospital. She didn't dare demand any more details. Not then, not in the years that followed. She felt sad—and very confused—whenever she thought about her little sister, but she knew it wasn't her place to ask her mom or dad to explain. They were her parents. All she could know was what they told her.

Growing up, I often wished I could be more like my adoptive parents. And not just because they were white, but because they possessed—outwardly, at least—what I saw as an enviable sort of nonchalance about my adoption. My father liked to answer especially nosy questions by saying, *If you put a Pole and a Hungarian together, you get a Korean! Where do you think they all came from?* My mother had the rare gift of making a person feel sorry they had asked, with little more than a hard, eloquent look. *For your sake,* her scornful expression seemed to say, *I will endeavor to forget this exchange ever happened.*

I wasn't like my parents. I couldn't turn other people's nosiness into a joke, and I couldn't make them regret it, either. Though it never seemed like the place or the time to offer an annotated personal history of adoption, when asked, I frequently did just that. I never even questioned why. It was the only way to make people understand, wasn't it? Yes, there were things I might never know about my origins, but I could do this much; I could explain it, capped with a smile, when people asked. I could let the story that had convinced me convince everyone.

But I did not have much to offer beyond a succession of half-guessed facts and a simple, happy ending. I was certainly not going to volunteer the fact that it hurt to know that I had been given up as a baby. It was a point of pride, I think, more than anything else. Why should strangers or even friends know just how often I thought about my birth family? Why should I give anyone a reason to feel sorry for me? I didn't know what to tell people about surviving a loss I couldn't even remember, or how the face I saw reflected in the mirror often seemed like a stranger's. And I couldn't lie to myself about why I struggled to feel I belonged in my own life; not since the day I'd finally asked a classmate why she didn't like me, and she pulled her eyes back and said, "The same reason no one else likes you." No matter how many answers I doled out or how much I prayed for acceptance, I was never going to grow out of being Korean in a white town. The truth was there not just in the daily torment of Catholic school, but in every "compliment" to my English, every question about where I was *really* from.

My parents, I assumed, would never accept this. To them, I was not *their Korean child*, I was *their child*, their chosen gift from God. They had waited so long and then they had gotten me, and there was no room in this radiant narrative to explain why I did not quite fit in. It would have felt like the greatest of betrayals to tell them I didn't belong in this place, this town, this *life*—all they would hear, I felt sure, was that I didn't think I belonged in our family.

It's unsurprising that a fanciful, weird, lonely kid like me would turn to stories, those already published and those yet to be written, in an attempt to flee the uncomfortable spaces I knew. When I felt unable to face my classmates at recess, I would usually ask to go to the library, where the school librarian would smile and point me toward the middle-grade shelves. The knot of tension in my chest eased as I paced the silent aisles, my eyes skipping from spine to spine. I lived through adventures pored over at the big wooden table behind the card catalog, through characters I considered friends—from Ramona Quimby and Sara Crewe to Meg Murry and Anne

Shirley. But as much as I loved these spunky literary heroines, they too were all white, and I couldn't see how I would ever find my way into lives like theirs. The only children's book I read in those years with an Asian American protagonist was *Farewell to Manzanar*, Jeanne Wakatsuki Houston's memoir about her family's incarceration at a Japanese American internment camp. In the TV shows and movies I watched, the classic films my mother and grandmother loved, people who looked like me were either invisible or presented for laughs—bowing and grinning, rarely speaking except with a heavy accent, sometimes even portrayed by white actors with exaggerated makeup and taped-back eyes. I knew I wasn't necessarily supposed to see myself in these laughable, silent, or tragic tropes, but they were all I had.

The stories I wrote throughout my grade school years were sites for my fledgling dreams of belonging. These invented worlds were another kind of refuge, but for a long time I had trouble locating myself in my own creations. Even when I was at my freest and most imaginative, peering beyond the limits of my own lived reality, I couldn't picture someone like me at the center of the story. When I tried to write novels, sprawled on my bed with a ballpoint pen and spiral notebook, I imagined girls who outsmarted grown-ups and rescued their best friends from kidnappers, girls who raced in the Iditarod and girls who traveled to worlds far beyond our galaxy—girls who were always white. To be a hero, I thought, you had to be beautiful and adored. To be beautiful and adored, you had to be white. That there were millions of Asian girls like me out there in the world, starring in their own dramas large and small, had not yet occurred to me, as I had neither lived nor seen it.

One spring when I was ten years old, my parents took me back to Seattle. I remember many steep walks up hills that week, stunning views of Mount Rainier rising over the city. Standing on the deck of a ferry and watching the foamy white cleft in the ship's wake widen as we lumbered toward land, I felt as though we were riding atop a skyscraper. My parents drove by the house whose attic apartment they had rented, and we slowed and lingered at the curb long enough for me to imagine my twenty-something father or mother peering down from the highest windows.

But my favorite outing of the week was to the Chinatown–International District and Uwajimaya, the enormous Asian supermarket. The cavernous store was so different from the Food-4-Less where we shopped for groceries at home; it was bursting with strange, wonderful smells, crammed with boxes and barrels of vegetables and fruits, tanks of live fish and still more seafood and meat on ice, jumbled displays of crockery and ceramics and lacquered chopsticks. While there were a hundred thousand things to touch and taste and try to take in, what truly enthralled me were the people: never before had I been entirely surrounded by Asians.

I had seen others, of course—one by one, back at home, and many more here in Seattle than in all the places we'd visited—but at this magical store they were everywhere: busy Asian shoppers hurried past us, clutching shopping lists; Asian grandmothers and aunties scanned products with a critical eye, weighed down by large purses; Asian parents pushed carts and strollers, towing their children by the hand. My mother and I cooed in unison over chubby-cheeked babies and toddlers with the same stick-up-straight, gravity-defying hair I had seen in my baby pictures—the hair that my mom had struggled with so, trying everything she could think of to make it lie down flat. "Don't you wish we could take one home with us?" Mom said to me. "A little brother or sister for you!"

At home, I kept a secret running tally of every single Asian person I had ever seen in public. I was on nodding terms with some of them: The woman at the Minute Market. The people who owned the Chinese restaurant. The couple who were always behind the counter at the Donut Den. It was possible to go months, even years without seeing any who were new to me. Walking around Seattle that week, I tried to play my Count the Asian game and lost track every time.

Here, finally, I was inconspicuous. There was no reason for anyone to look twice at me—though, in truth, a few passersby probably did glance at us, their eyes flicking over and up to my white parents and then back to my face. It was novel, exhilarating, to be one among so many; it was a glimpse of the world as it could be.

Why hadn't my parents raised me in a place like *this*? When I asked if we could move back here, I'm sure they thought I was kidding, but I wasn't. The seed of an idea, strange and hopeful, had been planted in my mind: there were real places, not far off in Korea, but here in my own country, where I could be just another face in the crowd.

I couldn't count all the Asians. But I quickly found another secret game to play. Although I believed that I would *never* meet anyone from my birth family—that, even if I did, it wouldn't be because they had recognized me wandering the streets of Seattle with my white parents—I spent the entire week scanning the faces of Asian people walking by. Every time we passed an Asian woman around my mother's age, I could not help but wonder if she might be my mother. A relative, at least, or perhaps just someone who'd known my birth family. They might still live here, all of them. I could not imagine passing a blood relation and remaining in total ignorance, our chance meeting neither sensed nor acknowledged by either of us.

If I walked by any of them on the street, I'd recognize them, wouldn't I? I would just *know*. In passing, I imagined, my birth mother and I would both suddenly be aware of a connection, unexpected and undeniable. Something in her would call out to me. I'd look into her face, overcome by a flash of familiarity, a memory woken. It seemed impossible that we would be able to cross paths like strangers and keep moving down the sidewalk away from each other, never to know, never to meet again.

Toward the end of our vacation, we visited the hospital where I had stayed as an infant. We had no actual business there, so I'm not sure how we ended up on the nursery floor, looking through a window at the rows of newborn babies in their plastic cots. Maybe my mother or father explained to the staff that I had been born there, that it had been my home for months while awaiting adoption. Standing before the newborns on the other side of the glass, Mom and Dad told me how they had rushed all the way, trying not to speed in the car. How they had met and talked with the doctors before grabbing my swaddled form from the nurse on duty, who cried as she said goodbye.

"What did the doctors tell you?" I asked, even though I'd heard the story many times before.

My mother recited the familiar litany of medical predictions. "But we weren't too worried about that," she said. "We had everyone we knew praying for you."

As I gazed at the babies in their hats and hospital-issue blankets, I thought about how I had started my life by proving these doctors wrong. My parents had not left everything to prayer; there had been a battery of screenings and tests when I was too young to remember, as well as a study of prematurely born children in which my mother made me participate around the age of three. The researchers quizzed me and the other children on shapes, colors, foods, and I answered every question incorrectly. I called a hamburger a hot dog, a circle a square; said, over and over, "I don't know," even though I did. My father would always laugh himself silly recalling every cheerful wrong answer I'd given the investigators. But I stumped them, he said, when they asked me to draw a picture. "Oh," I exclaimed, according to Dad, "I'll have to use my imagination!" And then I gave them my drawing and described it to them in detail, spinning the scene into a story. How, they wondered, could this poor child, who doesn't even know her colors, invent something like that on the spot? Where did her vocabulary come from?

Later, when Dad told Mom about my participation, she shook her head. It had never occurred to her that I would purposefully throw the test. When she asked me why, I told her I didn't like the people asking the questions. *They talked to me like I was stupid.*

As we made our way out of the hospital, I looked at everyone we passed in the pristine corridors, half hoping we'd run into a doctor my parents would recognize. My pediatrician at home was a woman, but for some reason I pictured this pessimistic know-it-all hospital doctor as a man. He would be wearing glasses, I decided, and he'd be walking briskly, eyes down, reading something on a clipboard, and my parents would stop him and say, *Oh, Dr. So-and-So, do you remember us? We came here to adopt this little girl in 1981!* The doctor would peer at me and ask how I was doing, and I would tell him: *I'm alive and completely fine, which just goes to show that doctors aren't always right.* He'd have the grace to look embarrassed; maybe he would even apologize. My parents would chime in with their usual line about prayer, angels watching over me, but the doctor and I would know the truth: I was not a miracle. I was a fighter. I was also lucky. And no one, no matter how smart or experienced, could expect to look at a tiny baby and know exactly who or what she would grow up to be.

For days and months afterward, for years, I would think about our visit to the city of my birth and wonder how a town I saw only through the eyes of a tourist could feel like home. After that trip, the idea began to grow in my mind that *I* had lost things, too, all those years ago when I was born too soon and my life changed course. These losses were not limited to personal history or the chance to know the people I'd come from. I had missed out on growing up in a place where my presence was not just accepted or tolerated, but a matter of course; where I might have heard others speaking my native language; where people like me were commonplace, not a wonder.

My parents had brought me to Seattle to show me where our stories had finally, fatefully converged, not to make me question the life that followed. And I didn't question it, not aloud. My rebellion was quieter, dreamy and ongoing and almost entirely page-bound. Writing was many different things: an outlet for experimentation, a means of wish fulfillment, a source of pride as I slowly improved and shared my stories with a couple of trusted teachers. But the most important thing my expanding creative life gave me as a girl, in terms of survival, was the permission to imagine a world I simply could not see in my white hometown. Only on the page could I build and live in a world that felt better, felt *right*. I was still alone at school, in my family, and in my town, but I could fill my notebooks with stories featuring some of my first Asian American characters. Childhood was perhaps something to be endured—but in adulthood, you got to choose your own setting, make your own story.

So I let my own characters grow up, though of course I knew almost nothing of the adult world, and I put them in hilltop houses and glamorous apartments in mostly unnamed cities, populating their lives and their workplaces and their histories with people of varying backgrounds, people who saw and understood them. At the time, I don't think I realized what a defiant and hopeful act it was to try to claim this kind of life for myself through the stories I made more and more my own. In most published stories, adoptees still aren't the adults, the ones with power or agency or desires that matter—we're the babies in the orphanage; we're the kids who don't quite fit in; we are struggling souls our adoptive families fought for, objects of hope, symbols of tantalizing potential and parental magnanimity and wishes fulfilled. We are wanted, found, or saved, but never grown, never entirely our own.

As a child, writing became my way to look ahead to the unknowable future, the one adoptees in stories so rarely get to have. To imagine that it would be *better* somehow. My parents might not have expected or fully understood it, but they did encourage it, buying me notebooks and then a series of old electric typewriters and pre-owned computers. They read what I deigned to show them and never complained about the hours I spent at work, imagining these other existences.

Turning to stories of my own imagination for refuge and rescue didn't mean I stopped wishing I were someone else, someone

41

white. That change would come later, and so gradually that I would never be able to name the precise moment when the old insidious desire evaporated. Nor did I gain any true sense of myself as Korean, in Seattle or at any point before adulthood; I still had no idea what it meant, or what I'd lost. If asked, I would almost certainly have refused to take Korean lessons or go away to adoption "culture camp," as some adoptees do now. I still did not *want* to be Asian if it meant being alone.

All the same, I found a measure of previously unknown power as I envisioned, in my own stories, places where someone like me could be happy, accepted, *normal*. My self-drawn heroines weren't alone, and I didn't have to be, either. Somewhere out there was the life I was meant for, a life I might find in time. It never seemed more possible than it did during the week I spent circling unfamiliar city streets crowded with other Asian Americans, my eyes drawn over and over to the faces of strangers as I looked for my people, for my parents, for a sudden light of recognition that never came.

T he lawyer who handled the adoption of Infant Girl Chung had known the birth parents, at least by sight, since before the adoption occurred. When she popped into their store once, several years later, the birth mother recognized her immediately. She greeted the lawyer by name, her voice low as she spoke from behind the cash register, and asked the same questions, over and over. *Do you know how she is? Do you know what happened to her?*

Kathy still hadn't had much experience with adoption. And this one, she recalled, had been a rather strange case. It had been classified as a "special-needs" adoption. It had been fast. And, not that it really mattered, she supposed, but the two families had been from such different worlds. The only thing they'd seemed to share was relief once the matter was settled.

She couldn't say how the girl was, or even where she was, not for certain; she hadn't kept in touch with the adoptive family. Even if she had, she couldn't pass along any information without the parents' permission. The mother, undeterred, said she wanted to see a photograph. She wanted to get in touch with the child and her parents. She wanted to speak with them, with her child. Would Kathy ask for her?

The lawyer had never expected any of the parents to request a change in the agreement. She could try to contact the adoptive parents, she told the birth mother, or forward a letter if they were still living at the same address. But the decision to allow contact was entirely theirs. Birth parents had no legal rights once an adoption was finalized. Even if all parties had agreed to a more open adoption arrangement at the time of placement—with, say, the exchange of regular letters, photos, and phone calls—the birth parents would have had to rely on verbal promises. The adoptive family had the right to cut off contact, at any time, with or without an explanation.

Kathy did send a letter explaining the birth mother's request. It was difficult to imagine the girl's adoptive parents viewing it as anything other than an attempted breach of their closed-adoption agreement. She couldn't imagine they would be pleased. She remembered how adamant they had been, throughout the adoption proceedings, about limiting any communication between the two families. They hadn't been able to hide their apprehension about the girl's birth family, hadn't even wanted to know her original parents' names. To them, the stability of the placement, the child's security and well-being, required the drawing of a hard, bright line between her family of origin and their own.

Weeks passed without any reply, and the wait did not surprise her. When Kathy finally received a response from the adoptive parents, it did not come as a surprise, either. Their report was so general it might have been about any child. Anyone.

She's doing well. She's healthy. She's an excellent student.

Kathy was welcome to share these updates with their daughter's birth mother, they said. They weren't comfortable sending any pictures.

Please, they added, *tell her we don't want to be in contact.*

D id you ever wonder how I ended up with you and Mom as my parents, and not someone else?"

My father and I were watching *SportsCenter* or *Baseball To-night*, sharing a pizza he had brought home after his closing shift at the restaurant he managed when I was in high school. I'm not sure what made me ask that evening—maybe I was just feeling philosophical. Like many people who know there is nothing for them in their hometown, I'd had one foot out the door all through high school. I might have been imagining those other, potentially more thrilling lives I could have led, now that the one I'd felt stuck in for so long was about to change course. "I mean, it's so random, don't you think?" I pressed him. "I could've been adopted by *anyone*."

My father has always been a joker, and it's a challenge for him to respond seriously, even to the most earnest questions. But this time, his answer was swift and sure, delivered with the ring of gospel truth. "God wanted us to have you," he said. "Too many things had to happen for us to adopt you. It never would have happened unless God planned it."

He recounted the familiar story of how Liz had learned about me, how she'd shared my story with my parents. Such was my parents' gratitude that they asked her and her husband to be my godparents; they met me just once, on the day they stood next to my parents in our town's only Catholic church and pledged to pray for me and help raise me in the Faith. I had always found it strange that I had this eternal connection to them, forged by chance and confirmed in the sacrament of baptism; that Liz, this messenger figure in family folklore, a person I could not even remember meeting, was in our lives just long enough to introduce my parents to me.

As Dad redirected his eyes to the parade of baseball highlights, I thought again of my godmother, the baptism captured in faded photos in a royal-blue album, and all the twists and turns that had led to my adoption. I'd been raised to believe in miracles, the handiwork of a loving and involved deity. My family's devout Catholic faith had often functioned as a kind of substitute for the Korean heritage I had lost, and I was very much under its sway: from Nativity plays and Lenten soup suppers to the holy cards stuffed in my Bible and the tiny cross my mother traced on my forehead before I went to school, there was rhythm and ritual in my Catholic upbringing, a sense of purpose and interconnectedness. I had long found comfort in it.

This wasn't the first time one of my parents had presented my adoption as a thing divinely ordered, almost biblical, though we all knew I hadn't been found in a watertight basket, plucked from the reeds. Now, when I considered all the factors, both known and unknown, that led to my adoption, I could no longer believe that anyone had planned it. I had always been told that my birth parents wished they had been able to keep me. If that were true, why didn't God care what *they* wanted?

Today I can understand why the idea of a providential adoption appealed to my parents. I've heard such sentiments echoed by adoptive parents over the years. Declarations like "We were meant to be" and "We were made for each other!" are not limited to romantic pairings; the words also ring true to many adoptive parents, religious or not, who cannot imagine their lives without their children. How many parents can? And who can question the rightness of a blessing sent from God?

If adopting a certain child is fated, ordained, it is easier to gloss over real loss and inequity, to justify the separation of a parent and a child. In my parents' case, I am sure that trusting in God's will for our family lent additional meaning to their long, sometimes painful wait to become parents.

But I think they also wanted to believe the Lord sent me to them because it was not always easy to know how to raise me. Even if we did not often talk about it, they knew that I struggled with not looking like them, that I had never quite felt I belonged in this place where I'd been planted. It must have been comforting, when they felt challenged or even lost, to believe that our family had been constructed by an all-knowing God, that it was predestined and so could not fail, no matter what.

I must have taken the box down again that day in high school because, after years of ignoring it where it gathered dust on the shelf, it had occurred to me that some of the words on those old, creased sheets of paper inside might make more sense than they had when I was a little girl.

The older I got, the less my parents and I felt the urge to retread what was, for us, ancient and settled history. But lack of conversation was not, on my part at least, lack of curiosity; while I did not often question aloud the foundational myth I'd been given, I was always alert for any clues that might fill in the gaps between guesses and facts. If my adoption was mentioned, I perked up, listening for a dropped hint, a new revelation.

And sometimes I also snooped. It was easy: our house wasn't large; none of us ever had much privacy. There were only so many places where my parents could attempt to store precious items, things of a sensitive nature. I knew that my mother kept her favorite pieces of jewelry, including the antique amethyst-and-garnet ring her aunt had given her, in the bottom compartment of a polished myrtlewood jewelry box. I knew that my father had a signed baseball, a box containing his only tie clip, and the strawberry-patterned dress I'd worn home from the Seattle hospital buried under a layer of socks in the top drawer of his dresser.

So of course I also knew about the ornately carved wooden box, about the same depth as a shoebox but twice as wide, up on a high shelf in their closet. When I was little, I pretended the box was a treasure chest; more than once I imagined burying it in the backyard and trying to convince the neighbor kids to follow a hand-drawn treasure map leading to it. I searched the box once while I was very young, disappointed to discover that it contained nothing more exciting than a pair of cufflinks my father never wore, my parents' marriage certificate, a few photos of my mom's late father and my dad's late mother, and papers that meant nothing to me.

When I decided to search it again, the first thing of interest was a slightly faded legal-size envelope buried among the photographs, stamped with a Seattle address. Inside was a bill for five hundred dollars and a business card that read:

KATHY L. SANDERSON
ATTORNEY-AT-LAW

Suddenly I felt like an amateur sleuth from one of the mystery series I'd read and loved as a child. But I wasn't Nancy Drew, girl detective, nor was I snooping into a stranger's secrets—this clue could lead me to information about my *own* life. My parents had told me that my adoption was handled by a private attorney, not an agency. Was this her?

A bill for five hundred dollars somehow seemed both too large and too small if what you were buying was a baby.

I wrote down the phone number of Kathy L. Sanderson, attorney-at-law, threw everything back into the box, and replaced it on the top shelf. Then I locked myself in the spare room, sat down on our lumpy blue futon, and reached for the phone I had bought in eighth grade with my saved-up allowance money. At the time I'd thought the phone was the height of cool: you could see rainbow wires and gears through the plastic outer shell of the receiver, and the numbers lit up when it rang. I dialed the number for Kathy L. Sanderson— nervously, guiltily, half an ear awake to the sound of one of my parents arriving home.

After a few rings, a woman answered, her voice cool and professional. "Kathy Sanderson's office."

"Hello." I sounded like a child, even to myself. "Is this Kath— Ms. Sanderson?"

"She's not in right now. May I ask who's calling?"

I gave my full name, spelling it out. She asked what the call was regarding. I wasn't sure whether the truth would serve me well, but it had taken all my nerve just to dial, and I couldn't think of a lie. "I think she handled my adoption in 1981," I said. "I wanted to ask her some questions about it."

My heart was racing. By now I felt less like a detective, more like a criminal. Should I just hang up? What was I going to say if Kathy Sanderson actually called me back?

A phrase, one I'd heard in the crime procedurals and court dramatizations I watched with my grandparents, skipped through my mind. *Attorney/client privilege.* She probably couldn't tell me anything. My parents had paid her five hundred dollars, and that made her their representative, not mine.

The woman didn't laugh or tell me to stop wasting her time. She dutifully took down our home number—another snag. I didn't have my own phone line; it was an expense my parents never would have considered. What would Mom and Dad think if Kathy called our home number and asked for me? As I hung up, I berated myself for acting so desperately.

Though I couldn't resist calling back once more, later that week or maybe the following, to leave another message, Kathy and I would not actually speak until many years later. She was my parents' faithful advocate to the last: when she did finally take my call, I believe with some reluctance, to answer every question I had, it was only because they had asked her to.

"Who was the attorney who handled my adoption?" I asked my mother with feigned calm, not long after my secret call to Kathy L. Sanderson's office.

"Kathy," she said, after a pause.

I noted the absence of a last name. Had she forgotten, or did she not want me to know?

"How much did you have to pay for my adoption?"

"It wasn't as much as it could have been, fortunately." My parents' income was a constant source of anxiety in our lives—also why I'd fretted about grades and test scores and financial aid for college since I was in junior high. "You know, you'd have been a steal at twice the price," Mom added.

If she was becoming suspicious, at least she was still talking. I asked if she or Dad had heard from the attorney at any point after my adoption. I waited for her to shake her head and say no, they never talked to the lawyer again; no, she had never come back with any more news for them. If they had learned anything more, heard anything more, wouldn't I already know?

"We heard from the lawyer once when you were younger," she said. As she spoke, her voice unusually hesitant, I realized I'd been holding my breath. "Your birth mother asked her to get in touch with us."

My birth mother had tried to reach out to us. To *me*. Of all the things I could have learned, this was the very last I expected. I felt like a puppet, pulled taut by invisible strings. All I could do was waver, wait to react to the next jerk, the next shock.

My mother continued chopping and stirring and preparing our dinner in the same kitchen I'd known all my life, with its dark brown paneling and the linoleum floor that was always a little sticky. From where I stood, I could see the old electric stove I hated to scrub, the white Formica table where we ate dinner most nights, and the sight of my mother calmly working on our meal after what she had revealed. It was her outward calmness that lit my fury and smoked my questions out. "What did she say? What did she want to know?"

"Your mother wanted to know how you were," Mom said. I was shocked—my parents never referred to my birth mother as *your mother*. "She wanted to know if you were all right. She asked for a picture of you. And . . . she said she wanted to talk to you, maybe see you in person."

The words fell like stones into a still pond, sending ripples of surprise and apprehension through the room. But I knew the possibility presented by my birth mother's curiosity must have been dead on arrival. My parents would have told her no.

We had never met, so they must have.

My mother confirmed that they hadn't been "comfortable" sharing photographs or detailed information. I was shocked by the casualness of her tone, whether or not it was assumed. She spoke as if we talked of my birth parents every day. As if it would mean nothing to me, this revelation that my birth mother had once tried to write to us. No, Mom said, she and Dad never seriously considered meeting her or allowing her to talk with me.

I could not picture such a conversation—a meeting?—taking place when I was little; the very idea frightened me a little. As a child, I recalled, sometimes I'd had nightmares about my birth parents showing up to take me with them. But whether it was in my best interest or not, now *or* then, I was upset that I'd never been allowed to decide for myself. Why couldn't we have talked on the phone, after we heard from my birth mother? Why couldn't my parents have allowed her—me—that much? I might have heard her voice. I might have heard her tell me, just once, that she had cared about me.

"We told her that you were happy and healthy," my mother volunteered. "We said you were doing well in school."

I nodded, though I hadn't been happy in grade school. Now, from a distance of some years, with good friends I loved and valued,

I could see even more clearly what a trial elementary school had been. I had been anxious every day; sometimes bullied, though my parents still didn't know the worst of it. I had been convinced that my biggest flaw, my physical appearance, was offensive and irredeemable. And while I was glad my birth mother didn't know about any of this—glad my parents hadn't told her the truth, because she had given me up so I would be happy—sometimes I wondered if I'd have had the courage to tell my Korean parents what I had never told my adoptive parents. I wondered if they might have understood me, or at least understood that pain, better than my white family.

"Where's the letter?" I asked. I *had* to see it. I could not understand why I hadn't. This was proof that my birth mother had cared. "I want to read it. *Now.* Was her name on it?"

Mom sighed. "If she signed her name, honey, I don't remember what it was. We don't have the letter anymore."

My age always shifts when I talk with my parents about the time my birth mother reached out to us. *You were five or six,* they'll say, or *maybe seven or eight?* The lawyer doesn't remember the year, either, though when we spoke she did remember meeting my birth mother and communicating her request to my parents.

There is much I cannot remember about my later conversation with my mother—my exact age; what my mom looked like at the time; if it was during or after her breast cancer scare during my sophomore year of high school, when I consciously tried not to argue with her because I'd faced the terrifying possibility of losing her; if I'd already begun looking ahead and applying to college and living with one eye always on the door. I don't remember the meal Mom prepared that night, or whether we all actually sat down together and ate it. But I remember her telling me that my birth mother had spoken of a sister when she met the lawyer again; I might even have *sisters,* she said, emphasizing the plural. *How many?* I asked. *How old are they? Why were they kept when I wasn't?* I will never forget the way my mother shook her head when I asked why she couldn't remember more; why she and my father had thrown away the only evidence of my birth mother's curiosity, her one and only attempt at contact. I remember her suggestion of a shrug, and the fact that while an explanation came later, there was never an apology. I remember how she wouldn't look directly at me as she said, simply, "It was a long time ago."

And though I pushed for more details about the letter itself—Was it typed or handwritten? Signed or anonymous?—neither of my parents would ever be able to remember anything else about it. I still don't know what I would have done if I'd been told about the attempted contact as a child. But I know I would have felt comforted. Maybe even relieved. Back then, the mystery I wondered about more than anything else was *why* my first parents had given me up. I knew some of the practical reasons: money, my health—but I did wonder if there were other reasons, too; if something about me had simply failed to move them, command their love or loyalty.

This is a question that, on one hand, makes little sense—many birth parents make the decision to place their children for adoption before they even give birth, and at any rate, what can a newborn or a small child do, or not do, to offend her parents? Yet when I talk with other adoptees, particularly those who don't know their birth families, I know I'm not the only one who's ever wondered: Was it something we did, as babies, as little children? Something we lacked that made us easier, possible, to part with?

I've never met an adoptee who has blamed their birth parents for their decision—we're more likely to turn inward, looking for fault. Growing up, I know it would have made an enormous difference to know that I was worthy of memory. That they still cared. That the adoption was *not* my fault. And although I learned of my birth mother's overture years too late to respond, I did feel better just knowing she had tried. I *wasn't* forgotten. Not entirely.

There was no way for me to contact them. My birth parents never got in touch with us again. Occasionally, though, after that day when I learned that my birth mother had tried, I would imagine a thick sheaf of letters meant for me, from different members of my birth family—handwritten letters filled with stories, pictures, questions about my life, words of love and curiosity. Letters that might have led me back to them.

Cindy was eleven when her parents ended their marriage. By then, Jessica was in college. Their mother moved to Oregon, where she had a cousin, and brought Cindy with her. After six months, Cindy asked to go live with her father. He didn't come for her himself—maybe he didn't want to see his ex-wife—but he said that she could come to him. A cousin was prevailed upon to drive Cindy back to Washington.

For days leading up to the move, Cindy was terrified her parents would change their minds; that her mother wouldn't let her go, or her father would say she had to stay. When it was finally time to leave, she grabbed her belongings—everything she had packed fit into a couple of plastic grocery sacks—and nervously bid her mother goodbye. They did not embrace. It would be many years before Cindy saw her again.

Her father remarried about a year after Cindy came to live with him, and his new wife was very kind. Still, Cindy had a difficult time adjusting to life with her father and stepmother. The three of them lived in a small condominium, perhaps nine hundred square feet, and she didn't have much space of her own. They had very high expectations—unrealistic ones, she sometimes thought. She was responsible for most of the cooking and cleaning while they both worked, and her father expected top grades. In her mother's home, she'd always had to sneak around to do her homework, but to her father—a writer and erstwhile scholar—education was paramount. She worked as hard as she could, but didn't always feel they approved of her. Cindy knew she was not allowed to complain. After all, wasn't life with her father and stepmother much better?

Her middle school, and the high school she attended for her freshman year, were very white. Cindy found a few good friends, but she knew she didn't quite fit in. When she did see other Koreans, often at church on Sundays, she didn't feel entirely at ease with them, either. There were so many things she wasn't supposed to talk about, even with supposedly close friends of the family: the divorce; her mother, and why Cindy didn't live with her; anything else that made her unhappy. She couldn't be real with anyone, couldn't show anyone who she truly was. She couldn't speak without hearing a parent's voice in her head: *What would people think? It's none of their business.*

After Cindy's freshman year, the family relocated to Guam, where her father had gotten a job with a relative's corporation. Now they lived in a two-story apartment complex, and most of their neighbors were Japanese. The few white people they knew were mostly military personnel and their families. Cindy found most of the island's residents friendly and fun to be around, more relaxed than the people she'd known back home. She had friends who were Guamanian and Chamorro, Filipino, Korean, and Japanese; who hailed from other islands, such as Yap and Truk and Palau. They'd hold fiestas where Cindy stuffed herself with pancit and lumpia, chicken kelaguen and pork adobo, as well as familiar favorites like kimbap and galbi.

She'd always lived in rainy northwest cities, but now she had to get used to a far more humid climate, and typhoons that battered the island every year. Before every storm in Guam, they would board up the windows, turn off the water and electricity, and collect water in large garbage cans for emergency use. Sometimes, depending on the might and duration of the storm, they'd have to go to the fire station and collect more water. Once the power was out for an entire month, and Cindy often cooked dinner on a single-burner propane stove.

Though she enjoyed her life in Guam, as high school graduation neared she found herself wondering what she ought to do next. How would she get to college, and who would pay for it? One afternoon, while watching television, Cindy saw an enlistment commercial featuring a young army officer scaling a rope over a rushing river. *I wonder if I could learn to do that*, she thought. She knew people in the army and navy, and thought the military would be both change and challenge—a way to meet interesting people and have adventures far from her parents' critical eyes, and eventually help her pay for school. The idea of being subordinate in a chain of command, of going where she was told and doing as she was ordered, didn't especially bother her. Hadn't she always been at the mercy of authority figures? At least in the army she would have hours off, the freedom to make some decisions on her own.

She went down to the recruiting office after school, all alone, and signed up. Her parents were shocked when she told them what she'd done; while her father had completed his mandatory military service back in Korea, serving as a KATUSA—a Korean Army attaché to the U.S. Army—that didn't mean he thought the army was the best choice for his daughter. *You won't make it*, he tried to tell her. *You'll wash out and you'll have to come back home.* But if her family still didn't know how strong or how determined she was, Cindy knew. She wanted to live on her own, see more of the world. She wanted to see if she could do something difficult, and do it well.

She completed basic training at Fort Jackson in South Carolina and Advanced Individual Training at Fort Lee, Virginia, before being assigned to Fort Carson in Colorado. From there she deployed to Cuba, Kuwait, and eventually to USAG Yongsan in Korea, where she would spend a year and a half serving in the country of her birth. It was her first time back in Korea since she'd left as a child.

Like most unmarried soldiers, Cindy lived on base, in the barracks, and shared a room with a fellow soldier from her company. There was always something to do, someone to meet, something new to learn, but she probably learned the most when she was off-duty and free to explore. Best of all, in her opinion, was the food: she found food stands that sold ddukbokki, bbundaegi, and fish cakes and took every opportunity to indulge in jjajangmyeon—her favorite comfort food. Cindy was fascinated by everything in Korea, especially all the Korean people. Sometimes she was filled with an undeniable sense of homecoming, or maybe just a sharp longing for it, yet she knew she was no longer Korean *enough* to belong here. She was an outsider, an American, and had been for a long time.

While she was stationed in Korea, her father's mother—who still lived there—passed away, and Cindy asked for leave to attend the funeral in Incheon. She welcomed the opportunity to reconnect with relatives who hadn't seen her since she was a baby, but it was a strange visit, too; she had forgotten many of them, and assumed many had forgotten her. She did not get to stay with them long enough, or learn as much about them as she would have liked.

For eighteen months, she lived at Yongsan and reveled in being back in her mother country. She squished into Seoul's buses and subway cars and went out looking for novelty and adventure every chance she got. Sometimes she traveled around with a friend and fellow Korean American army specialist who also had personal reasons for wanting to be stationed at Yongsan—she had been adopted at the age of twelve, she explained to Cindy, and she'd always been curious about the people she'd left behind. Cindy knew her friend spent many off-duty hours searching for clues about her biological family. She wondered what it would be like to be of Korea, a long-lost daughter of the place, and know even less about your Korean family than Cindy knew about hers.

I did not expect anyone from the adoption organization to return my call. I had stumbled across their website and requested an informational interview, though I did not even know to call it that—I just asked if anyone there had time to meet with me. Later I couldn't even understand why I'd done it. Why was I looking for an opportunity to talk with strangers about adoption? Shouldn't I have wanted to steer clear, after all the questions I'd had to answer as a child?

I had been out of my parents' home for five years, out of college less than a year. I wasn't sure what I wanted to do in the long term, but I could not see myself in corporate life and I wasn't quite ready to apply to graduate school. I *had* always been interested in adoption stories, and had by then even met a couple of other adult adoptees— including a college friend from the Midwest whose self-possession and adoption-related nonchalance I genuinely envied. I didn't know anything about adoption or foster care policy; I had only my own experiences to draw on, but I had spent my entire life trying to help other people understand adoption so they would accept me and my family. Perhaps now I could help address those gaps in knowledge on a much larger scale. If families like mine were better understood, if more people knew that adoption was far more complicated than common media portrayals might suggest, maybe fewer adopted kids would have to answer the kinds of questions I had gotten, or feel pressured to uphold sunny narratives even they might not necessarily believe in.

I took the entry-level position offered to me. After a lifetime of feeling isolated by my adoption, I began to think of myself as part of a broader culture of people affected by it. I could ponder and discuss its complications in ways I could never have done while under my parents' roof, talking with people who knew more about the practices and policies than I did. On my own time, I researched what reunions typically involved and read blog posts and articles by adoptees and birth parents. I began connecting with and chatting with more adoptees, including some who were in open adoptions or had found their birth families.

"I've always been interested," said one woman who had been adopted as a child. Her original parents, like many around the world, hadn't realized their daughter could be sent to live with people in another country when they placed her in an orphanage due to desperate hardship. "My curiosity was repressed for years, because I just wanted to fit in with everyone else and feel 'normal,'" she told me, an admission I well understood. "But I never fully let go of my past."

I also spoke with birth parents in open adoptions, including a birth mother who had placed two children for adoption and later found both of them. She had become a therapist, focusing on adoption and family therapy. "I think that other than giving birth to my children, reunion was the most upending, surreal experience of my life," she said. "If you do search for your birth family someday, don't rush things. Just like any relationship, it's delicate, and it should be allowed to grow and build as naturally as possible." While this advice seemed sound, I still could not imagine meeting or talking with anyone in my birth family.

Others I talked to freely offered their opinions about adoption and whether I should attempt to open up my own. One adoptee said, "Closed adoptions like ours are little better than child trafficking," and another said, "I've really never thought about searching. I never think about my birth family at all." One adoptive parent shocked me by saying, "I can't imagine what my son would gain from knowing his birth mother; she has so many problems"; but another, a social worker who had an open adoption with his child's birth family, said, "If you ever *do* decide to search for them, your birth parents will find a daughter they can be very proud of"—a kindness I never forgot. One person told me, "It's usually unhappy adoptees who search; you probably haven't because you're so well adjusted!" and another person told me, "You should find your birth mother and let her know that you're okay. I'll bet she thinks about you every day."

It was this last comment I held in my mind, turning it over and over, sometimes with deep skepticism, sometimes with a longing I could not deny. Did she still think about me? It seemed too much to presume. Why should she? What about me was so worthy of daily remembrance, especially when she'd never had the chance to *know* me?

Even if she did think about me, I knew I wasn't ready to look for her. I wasn't sure I ever would be.

I don't remember the exact day I learned there was another way to get more information *without* a search or a reunion, but as soon as I did, I thought about it almost nonstop. In many states, "nonidentifying information"—the brief social history of an adopted person's biological parents, as much as they'd wanted to share at the time of placement—was kept on file and made available to any party to a closed adoption. I had never known that *any* information could be requested in closed adoptions like mine without opening records or appealing directly to the birth parents. One person requested information, and a neutral and uninvolved party responded: what could be simpler?

A few weeks after my twenty-fourth birthday, I wrote a short letter to the King County Court in Seattle and requested all available nonidentifying information about my birth family. As I signed and sent it, I felt thankful that I could take this step—so benign, barely a baby step!—without stirring up anyone's secrets or intruding in anyone's life. I told no one about my decision to request the information. Not my friends, not my parents, not even my husband, Dan. If they knew, I thought, they would ask me if I wanted to find my birth family. And how would I answer?

I never wanted or set out to begin in secrecy, or withhold part of myself from the people who cared about me. But long after the papers are signed and the original familial bonds are severed, adoption has a way of isolating the adoptee. For me, it had always been this way: a wide sea seemed to separate the lone island of my experience from the well-mapped continents on which other people, other families, resided. Despite how well my husband knew me, despite all of our conversations about our respective childhoods, I didn't think even he could possibly understand how much my adoption had given me; how much it had taken away.

The creased self-addressed envelope, freshly stamped in green with the county seal, arrived weeks sooner than I had expected. Inside I found two pieces of paper. Spanning one single-sided page was a profile of my birth parents; someone had transcribed bullet points of information, no doubt gathered by form, into short, choppy sentences. I read with heart pounding, hands trembling, though my eyes were as clear and dry as the list of facts. My birth mother was nine years younger than my birth father. She was five feet two and a half inches, and he was five feet seven and a half. Both were described as having "Korean features." She had a high school degree; he was "a good student" who had gone to college and graduate school. Their religion was listed as Christian. They had come from Seoul, and both were "in good health" at the time of placement. They had other children—daughters, the form stated—whose names weren't listed.

I must have read the single sheet ten times or more before letting it fall to the desk. I had expected to feel excited, to be *moved*, no matter how much or how little I learned. In a way, it was a wealth of information—so much more than I'd ever had. But somehow the brisk, bare-bones facts seemed as cold and uninspiring as the database from which they had likely been retrieved. Holding it, reading it, left me feeling empty.

On the second sheet of paper was a list of confidential intermediaries and an explanation of their role: for a fee, a third party could make contact with my birth parents and deliver a letter on my behalf. If I did want to learn more, if I wanted to ask any more questions, this was the only path forward.

I would have to ask them.

I considered this. It was one thing to petition some nameless, faceless county employee to spend a few minutes mining long-forgotten facts from a file drawer. It was another to address my birth parents directly, reminding them of an event—a person—they might not have talked of in years. They knew nothing about me; I was a stranger. They owed me nothing. Wasn't that the whole point of my adoption? What right did I have to contact them, let alone ask them for anything?

When I showed Dan the letter, he was surprised that I'd sent away for the information, though to his credit he did not ask why I'd initially kept it from him. His innocent reaction confirmed my fears: hadn't this decision been entirely out of character, the last thing anyone would have expected me to do? Would others be surprised, too, if they knew I'd gone looking for more? I imagined my adoptive parents' reactions, and wondered if even this tiniest of steps had been disloyal.

Dan asked if I was glad to know more about my birth family. "It's not very much," I pointed out.

"But if you want to find out more about them, at least now you know how."

I shook my head, as much in disbelief at my own choices—*why*

64

had I gone looking, anyway?—as a rejection of his words. The idea of searching for my birth family, of talking to or even meeting them, felt less like betrayal now that I was grown up and out of my parents' house. But I had always told everyone that one family was enough. My adoptive parents were my real parents; that was it.

Though there was still so much to learn, could I be content with the information I already had? Dan was applying to graduate schools in several different states, and I knew we would likely be moving within the year—this was not the time to upend our lives by launching a reckless search for my birth family.

But I kept the letter. When we moved the following year, I made sure to bring it with us.

I n the late summer of 2007, in a small antiseptic-
scented exam room in North Carolina's only free-
standing birth center—a room just large enough
for two chairs, an exam table, a wash station, and a padded swivel
stool—my husband and I sat with a midwife who checked boxes
and scribbled notes while we talked. Her low voice was friendly, if
tired; she had been up all night with a laboring mother. I sat under
the fluorescent lights, anxiety twisting through my excitement as we
made our way through the patient forms. I was happy, and at the
same time I did not feel ready.

The midwife's questions started out easy enough: When was my
birthday? Was this my first pregnancy? How far along did I think I
was? I answered quickly; I knew the sooner we completed the forms,
the sooner we could listen to the heartbeat.

But when she asked me how many brothers and sisters I had, I
hesitated. I didn't know how to answer. This was a simple question,
wasn't it? The obvious reply—and true in its way—would be "zero."
I had been raised an only child. My entire biological family was contained, right here, within my own body.

Yet ever since I was a little girl, I'd been told my birth parents likely had other children. The lawyer had mentioned a sister, and the limited birth family social history I'd received a couple of years earlier had confirmed that my birth parents did have other daughters when I was born. I still did not know their exact ages, their names, or anything more about them, but that had not stopped me from trying to imagine them—sisters who would have known me, grown up with me, if not for my adoption.

The midwife was still waiting patiently, and now, beneath my indecision, I was aware of another kind of fear. "I'm adopted," I said. It sounded like an apology, even to my ears. I felt even worse.

She asked if I knew how old my mother—*sorry, your birth mother*—was when I was born. I shook my head. How about the birth itself? Did I have any record of how it went? I told her about my premature arrival, the two and a half months I spent in the hospital. When I said, a little panic crowding my words together, that I didn't know about any pregnancy complications or illnesses that ran in the family, didn't even know what had caused my mother's early labor, the midwife looked up from her clipboard with a gentle smile. When it came to pregnancy, she said, some things could be hereditary. Knowing how it went for my mother might help us guess how things would go for me. But if I didn't have that information, that was fine; we'd just make do without it.

Her voice was calm, confident—a voice anyone would find reassuring in the throes of labor. Still, I felt uneasy as I watched her skim, then skip the rest of the questions.

Everything I knew of my life began on the day I was adopted. It was as if I had simply sprung into being as the five-pound, chubby-cheeked two-month-old my parents picked up at the hospital. I'd always found it difficult to imagine my birth mother pregnant with me, difficult to grasp that my existence had been entirely dependent on a woman I would never know. In all the years I had spent thinking about my birth family, my thoughts had rarely turned to unknown facts about my mother's pregnancy. I was young and healthy; I hadn't yet begun to worry about aging, illness, genetics catching up with me. When I pictured my birth mother, I did not picture her pregnant. I pictured her holding me and saying goodbye.

Now that *I* was pregnant, those mysterious months my birth mother had spent carrying me suddenly seemed far more important. What *had* pregnancy been like for her? Why had she gone into labor so early? What if the same thing happened to me?

Dan and I had moved to North Carolina in 2005 just days after our second anniversary; he was a doctoral student, I was the bread-winner, and we were first-time homeowners. Like my own parents, we had married very young. Well-meaning questions and criticism, even the knowledge that we were severely alarming some of our rel-atives, only hardened our resolve.

For me at least, the concept of family had always been deter-mined and defined by the actions of others. By the time I reached adulthood, I had been geographically and financially indepen-dent from my own parents for four years, and possessed an only child's overgrown sense of confidence in my choices combined with an adoptee's innate belief that family was something you *made*—something you built through sheer force of will. As a young woman, I wasn't afraid of getting married, nor was I afraid of remaining single; what I feared was the threat of passivity—being powerless, like I had been as a baby, to determine my own future.

We probably *should* have been more afraid to bet on our young marriage, but we were too young to have built up a real fear of commitment or change; too trusting and sure of each other to doubt that we'd make it. We have been married for fourteen years. When we talk about it now, we are quick to laugh and admit that it *could* have been a disaster. It's funny only because it worked out; because we have been together, and lucky, for so long.

By the spring of 2007, when Dan and I began talking about starting a family, we were still very young, but felt we'd had enough time to ourselves. He was halfway through his PhD program, and we had enough money to pay our mortgage, travel, save a little, and fill the house we'd bought with carefully selected furniture and two cats. I'd been considering applying to creative writing programs, something I had never quite felt ready to do before, and had joined a local writing group so I'd have deadlines and an excuse to work on the stories saved on my hard drive.

Then I found I no longer had the energy to write in the evenings or sit through long workshop sessions with the group. The reason for my sour stomach and deep exhaustion should have been obvious, but for days I remained in deep denial. Dan and I had been saying *Maybe now* would *be a good time . . .* for only two or three months. We weren't even trying. We had barely stopped *not* trying.

I had just assumed it would take longer.

One morning a few months after my twenty-sixth birthday, I found my husband rinsing his cereal bowl in the kitchen sink, getting ready to leave for campus. I had been staring at the white stick in my hand for what felt like hours, though it could have been only a few minutes. It had taken some time for the disbelieving fog to lift; for my brain to nudge me into action and my shaky legs to carry me downstairs. When Dan turned around, a question in his eyes, I held up the test.

"Does this look positive to you?"

In the birth center, the midwife pulled out a new batch of forms and turned to my husband. Dan was so obviously his parents' child. A quarter inch shy of six feet—exactly his father's height—with his mother's wide smile and dark curly hair, a scientist in a family of teachers and more scientists, he could trace half of his family back to county Cork in Ireland, and had grown up hearing stories about the bakery his Lebanese grandparents had owned. Like most people I knew, Dan couldn't understand what it felt like to lack any and all knowledge of the people who'd created you; to grow up with a family you loved but could never quite recognize. I envied how his answers came so easily, one after another.

Finally the midwife set down her clipboard and suggested that we have a listen to the heartbeat. The paper stretching over the exam table rustled as I clambered up. Dan's hand closed around mine; he smiled, as excited as me. This was the moment we'd been waiting for, the moment that I knew would make the weeks of morning sickness and wrung-out exhaustion worth it. The midwife turned on the fetal ultrasound and ran the wand over the slope of my lower belly. We listened to the low hum of the monitor.

"I think the baby's hiding." She didn't sound concerned, but I felt a stab of fear. *What if there's no heartbeat?* There was so much we couldn't see, couldn't control, and I had no idea what to expect. Though I couldn't know it yet, I would come up against this uncertainty over and over again, even though mine turned out to be an easy, low-risk pregnancy.

Whirrwhirrwhirrwhirr.

Quiet, pulsing, the rhythm seemed almost too fast. But it *was* a rhythm, steady and sure. "Is that—?" I began, just as it disappeared.

All I wanted was to hear it again.

I held my breath as the wand moved again over my stomach. *Come on, baby.* The midwife pushed a little harder and turned up the volume, and the *whirr* suddenly turned into a loud *whumpwhumpwhump.*

"Sounds perfect!" she beamed. "About one hundred and sixty beats a minute. Just what it should be." Seeing the awed look on my face, she laughed and added, "It's real, I promise."

"It's working so hard," Dan said.

The three of us fell silent, listening to that strong and unmistakable rhythm. It was the single best sound I had ever heard.

Our growing family was more than a wish or a far-off possibility; it was *real,* the strong heartbeat a thrilling introduction. Our child was racing toward life. Toward us. The wonder and love I felt was the same known by countless mothers before me. I found that thought comforting, somehow—in this, at least, I was *normal*. I still had trouble thinking of myself as anyone's biological anything, but loving this baby would be the easy part. It would come naturally. And when our child was born, I wouldn't be alone anymore. There would be someone who was connected to me in a way no one else had ever been.

My eyes settled on the print hanging across the room. A woman, black-haired like me, cradled her pregnant belly, gazing down at it with a tender expression. The painting so strongly depicted that physical link, the original connection between parent and utterly vulnerable child. It had always been such a mystery to me—here I was now, in its thrall, and still I couldn't comprehend it. I pulled my shirt back down and slid my feet to the floor. "Nine months seems like a long time, but it's really not," the midwife told us. "You'll be meeting this baby before you know it."

I was going to be a mother. Someone would depend on *me*. Our relationship would last for the rest of my life; though it had yet to begin, I could not imagine it ending. Yet that was exactly what had happened to the bond between me and my first mother: it had been broken. We had both survived it, learned to live apart, and while I *knew* this—had known it for as long as I could remember—it had never struck me as unnatural until I heard my own child's heartbeat.

Dan and I had our lives to ourselves now, but soon that would change. As incredible as it had been to hear the heartbeat, to realize that we would soon be parents to a real baby, for me our first pre-natal appointment had opened up a new source of worry and doubt. Yes, I had to give birth, make sure I was prepared for it. But that was only the beginning. What questions would our child have for me about our family? How could I help them understand and feel connected to their history and heritage when to me it was still little more than a fable? So far, I'd been asked just a few pages' worth of family information, and I hadn't been able to supply it.

As we left the birth center, I couldn't shake the overwhelming feeling that our baby was destined to inherit a half-empty family tree. I wasn't even a mother yet, and already the best I could offer was far from good enough.

When I was young, my family's view of adoption as identity trump card—more powerful than blood, or appearance, or the bigotry I encountered—made it nearly impossible to imagine, let alone talk about, a future reunion with my birth family. I always understood that my parents didn't want me to search. Or perhaps it's more accurate to say I understood that they didn't want *me* to want to search. I was enough for them, and they wanted to be enough for me.

But they had also pledged not to stand in my way if I ever decided to find my birth family. When I asked them a version of the question I heard from my first-grade classmate—though of course I wouldn't have dreamed of using his term, *real parents*—they always said, "You can look for your birth parents someday if you want to. When you're grown up." And so I understood that it was not a decision for a child like me to make, but one for a mature and responsible adult.

We rarely talked about how or why I might search one day; I was left to ponder this on my own, with the occasional and unreliable supplement of television shows and novels. The few adoption stories

I read or saw on TV always seemed to end with the adoption of a child, the focus on the loneliness and destitution from which the child had been saved. If it was a dramatic reunion story, it might end when the adoptee and birth parent (usually the birth mother) found each other—or with the adoptee standing on a stranger's doorstep, bravely smiling through tears as the door swung open to reveal the unsuspecting parent. In the case of several *Masterpiece: Mystery!* installments I watched with my mother and grandmother, embittered adoptees whose origins had been carefully hidden—sometimes, even from them—came back as adults to murder their original parents.

Few of these movies or shows or novels ever showed what happened *after* the tears or the hugs or the accusations, when people had to cope with new knowledge, to move forward—and choose whether to build a relationship from nothing since the moment of rupture. That was always the part that intrigued me, the part I found so difficult to imagine. Even as a child, I understood that the easy, heartwarming happy ending was the kind of adoption story most people wanted to see. If this realization caused me a slight squirm of discomfort (was that not what my own story recalled, as it was often told to me?), I saw the appeal of such simplicity—though I still longed for stories in which the unvoiced questions, the quiet drama of the everyday adopted experience, did not remain so unexplored.

I remember a few months before I left for college, Mom and I were driving home from an appointment when she told me that the son of a family friend, Jason, had recently reunited with his birth family. I hadn't even known he was adopted. "He's not coming home for Christmas," Mom told me. "He's decided to spend the holidays with his birth mother and her other kids. His mother is heartbroken."

Jason's adoptive mother apparently believed her son was upset with them, and that was why he wasn't coming home this year. I tried to picture Jason, whom I'd seen perhaps once or twice. He was older than me by a few years. I felt a twinge of envy that, as a white kid, he could fit in everywhere *and* pass for his parents' biological son. And now he had found his birth family, too.

"Why is his mom so upset?" I asked, though of course I knew. I believed my mother had no business endorsing what I saw as unreasonable levels of parental sensitivity—she ought to take Jason's side, or at least try to talk his mother down. I could see why Jason had waited until he was no longer under his parents' roof to reunite with his biological family. On the heels of this thought came another, more traitorous and vindictive: *If his parents can't handle the thought of him ever knowing his birth family, maybe they shouldn't have adopted him in the first place.*

"I'm sure Jason's birth mother would love to have a relationship with him," Mom said. "But what if that's not *all* she wants?"

She told me she'd heard "lots of stories" about kids who found their birth families and tried getting to know them. And then it had turned out their birth parents were more interested in getting their hands on their adoptive family's money. She sounded more regretful than judgmental, but I knew we were no longer talking about Jason, or whether his birth mother's motives were mercenary or pure. This, I understood, was a message for me.

I wanted to tell her I knew what she was implying, and why. But with the heartless, deadeye aim of a teenager, I also knew I could say something that would upset her more than a direct challenge of the facts. "Jason's parents shouldn't make him feel guilty for choosing to spend *one* holiday with the woman who gave birth to him," I said. "She's his mother."

Mom's mouth flattened into a hard line. I could tell she was annoyed now, maybe even hurt, but she absorbed the hit. "I suppose," she said.

As we drove on in silence, I almost regretted ending the conversation so defiantly. I wanted to ask if she knew *how* Jason had found his birth mother, or if she had found him. To me, his adoptive parents' fears seemed unfounded—how could she possibly lose her son to his birth family? If I ever found mine, I assumed our relationships would resemble pleasant, long-distance friendships. They would never be my refuge, my first call in a crisis. Even if you found your birth family, how could you ever be certain they would stick around? How could you think of them as your *real* family when they hadn't been there all along?

For years I had wondered what my own adoption reunion would look like if it ever came to pass. I still didn't feel like the adult I knew I would have to be before I considered a search. Yet in a few months I would leave for a college three thousand miles away. Though I was anxious about it—I had long thought of myself as a homebody, and not a terribly brave one at that—I was eager to move "back east," as my parents called it, and be on my own. If this was not an acceptable time to consider a search, perhaps that time was drawing near. Would my family support me, as they'd always promised, if that was what I chose? Or would they try to talk me out of it?

In the days following our first prenatal appointment at the birth center, my mind never strayed far from the court letter with its accompanying list of intermediaries, both stuffed in a folder at the back of our filing cabinet. Though I had long since memorized every line, every fact in the letter from the county adoption office, I found and read it again.

The timing for a birth family search was no better than it had ever been. I had no idea if it would be possible to find them. Even if I did, what would happen then? How did one go about talking to such close and distant relations? How to restore connections and relationships that were never meant to be broken in the first place?

I didn't know if the discoveries would change how I thought about my parents, or the new family Dan and I were just beginning. To upend our hard-won stability by adding any unknown variables might well be foolhardy. Yet ever since the birth center, my mind had been hijacked: What if I *did* find my birth family? What if I ended up with a richer and more complete story to share with my children, one that would finally unfurl all the branches on my family tree? I could see the faces of my closest relatives. I could know their names. What else might I gain—for me, yes, but also for my future child—if I just stopped being so afraid?

This had always been a possibility, even if it had seemed far-fetched. I had considered it before, made calls, researched what it would involve. My adoptive parents *had* told me a search was something I could pursue on my own, one day, if I chose to. As a child, of course, that was rather like hearing them say I could become an astronaut or a famous actor or an Olympic athlete—possible, perhaps, but highly improbable. Now I forced myself to acknowledge just how simple it could be: my birth parents weren't in hiding. Reconnecting would not require a miracle, a private investigator, or a talk show chasing drama for ratings. It would be a matter of pushing some paper around. One letter, one phone call, was all it might take.

Of course, there were risks. My birth parents might not want to talk to me. I might not like what I found. And I still felt it was not my place to make demands of them. It would be terrible to be given up all over again, when I was old enough to understand the rejection.

Then, too, I knew my decision would surprise many people, including some who had known me for most of my life. I could barely imagine explaining this to my husband. How would I tell my adoptive parents? My friends from college, my friends from home? I'd been so insistent in my declarations about the goodness of adoption and how nothing was "missing" from my life. I'd have to brace for my parents' reactions; for all the people who might say, *I thought you said you didn't care about meeting your birth family.*

That was my old line from childhood, one of so many I'd faithfully learned, one I'd used to deflect the notice and the nosy questions I had not wanted to answer. Maybe it was also what I had long believed. But people changed their minds—people changed *themselves* all the time, for all sorts of reasons. And my biggest reason was approximately the size of a plum, twelve weeks now and counting.

This realization welled up, overflowing in another discovery: I had nothing to prove any longer. Even if I still felt the need to assert my love for my adoptive parents, or defend my family to people who had no idea how it felt or what it meant to be adopted, that did not mean I had to forever deny all interest in the people who'd given me life. It was time to lay down the burden of being "the good adoptee," the grateful little girl who'd been lost and then found. Who cared what anyone thought of my decision? Who cared about their questions?

The most important question *now*, the one I was finally ready to ask, was so urgent I almost felt I could see it, suspended in the air; hear it whispered in my own voice.

What do you want?

I wanted to find them.

All the doubts, the risks, my fear about what people might think or say fell away as I faced this truth. And I knew it was right; there was no need to ask myself again. I felt shaken, but absolutely sure. This hadn't always been my answer—perhaps even now it wasn't the best or the smartest one. But it was what I wanted.

I wanted to write to them.

I wanted to know everything they were willing to tell me.

How much had my birth parents struggled when making the decision to place me for adoption? How did they feel about it now? How much might I resemble my sisters? What would it be like to meet them, to hear a voice or look into a face that was like my own?

I wondered how often my birth family talked about me—if they ever prayed for me, or wished for some way to know that I was all right. Suddenly very little seemed to separate us. And maybe that had always been true, especially if they really had cared about me; if they had known me once. As my thoughts reached out to them, all at once I could envision hundreds of gossamer-thin threads of history and love, curiosity and memory, built up slowly across the time and space between us—a web of connections too delicate to be seen or touched, too strong to be completely severed.

Part II

So, you're looking for a search angel?"

According to Washington State law, under which I was placed for adoption in 1981, adoption records are now part of the public record. An adopted person can request a copy of the original birth certificate, on which the birth parents' full names appear, and use the information to find them. Birth parents and other parties to adoption who don't want their information released by the state can file a contact preference form stating as much. But legislation opening most Washington State adoptions went into effect only in July 2014. At the time I searched, my adoption records had to be accessed and shared with me by a confidential adoption intermediary, and then only after my birth family approved the information exchange. The policy made a kind of sense to me back then, though I now believe that access to basic information about one's origins, especially crucial medical and social history, is a right no state should limit.

When I searched, the intermediary represented one more hurdle, and an expensive one at that. Researching the process, I learned that many intermediaries called themselves "search angels," perhaps because it made their role sound largely altruistic. The term called to mind search-and-rescue volunteers, the patron saint of lost items, or perhaps a religious-leaning matchmaker. I could never bring myself to use it without a slight eye roll.

"I've been a search angel for years. I think of it as my vocation," the first intermediary I spoke with told me over the phone. "I charge five hundred dollars up front, and five hundred once I get your adoption file for you."

"How did you get into this"—I almost said "business," but despite the mention of her fee, that word didn't seem quite right—"service?"

Her story came pouring out: like many single women facing unplanned pregnancy in past decades, she was pressured to let her child be adopted by a couple who could provide "a better life" and allow her to "move on" with hers. She always regretted the decision, and as she told me this, I felt sorrowful and angry on her behalf.

"When I found my child, she wasn't ready to see me at first. I kept calling until she agreed to meet," she said. At this, I began to feel uneasy. Is that what she would do with my birth parents? She proudly told me that she had facilitated five hundred reunions, and I got the distinct feeling she already thought of me as Reunion Number 501.

"I'm very open to meeting my birth family," I told her. "But if they don't want to be in contact, I'll respect that. I don't want them pressured in any way."

"So what you're saying is you're *healthy*," she laughed. I felt stung, and rather alarmed. "Good for you!"

I had a brief vision of this person ringing up my birth parents—or just showing up on their doorstep!—intent on coaxing them into a reunion with the daughter they had not seen in nearly twenty-seven years. She might imply that they owed me a meeting for the sake of my personal healing; never mind their shock, or what they actually wanted. Did my own feelings and wishes matter to her? Or would I be just another tally mark in her book of saved lives?

I worked my way down the list. There was the man who told me he pitied people like me with our "prehistoric" closed adoptions, and the woman who said I had no business writing to my birth family unless I was ready to fly out and meet them immediately: "Think of how it would make them feel if you sent a letter and didn't even want to *see* them!" There was a social worker and fellow adoptee who seemed compassionate and understanding, but after our first conversation I never heard from her again. I desperately wanted to hire someone who would listen, understand the unique circumstances of my placement, and see us all as individuals with our own feelings and histories to be respected. Did an intermediary exist who wouldn't view my birth parents or me as a cause?

Weeks into my search for an intermediary, I began to wish it were possible, and legal, for me to acquire my birth parents' contact information and reach out to them myself. It would be terrifying, I knew, and perhaps they would have a harder time refusing me than an intermediary if they wanted to cut off contact, but at least I trusted *myself*. I did not trust any of the strangers with whom I'd spoken.

Finally I received a call back from an intermediary named Donna, for whom I'd left a message weeks earlier. She told me she was relatively new to search-angel work. We chatted for an hour. Donna was taken aback, as many other intermediaries had been, because I was not writing to specifically ask for a meeting right away. But she did agree that, in principle, it was better not to press or demand; when the time came, we would proceed slowly and carefully with my birth parents.

In the blessed nonqueasy, high-energy days of my second trimester, I sent Donna a deposit and a notarized form authorizing her to petition the court for my sealed adoption file. She told me it would be several weeks before we heard anything. "I'll call you as soon as I have it in my hands," she promised.

Dan had been surprised again when I told him about my decision to search for my birth parents while pregnant, and this worried me. If he could not understand the choice I had made, I felt sure no one else would. But his surprise soon made way for happiness and questions about the search and the intermediary's role and how I felt about the prospect of finding my parents—and my sisters.

"You know, I always picture your sisters as older versions of you," he said. "No matter what, it would be so amazing if you could meet them!"

For weeks, while I waited for Donna to complete the bureau-cratic slog and secure my adoption file, Dan had been the only person in my life who knew all about my search, as well as the reasons for it. I didn't want well-meaning friends checking up on my progress, asking whether I'd found or heard from my birth fam-ily. I especially did not want my parents' words of—hurt? caution? fear?—rattling in my brain as I waited. So my own search for truth included this early lie of omission: I did not tell them I was looking for my birth family because I wanted to *find* them and perhaps be in contact. Instead I said that I had hired an intermediary to request an updated medical history on my behalf, and let my parents believe this was all I wanted.

They were still surprised; I was pregnant, after all, and I had a lot going on, didn't I? I expected more questions, perhaps an open objection to my plan. When they told me on the phone, "Okay, let us know what you find out," I wondered if their expressions matched the calmness of their words.

I tried not to recall the cautionary tales they'd told me about adoptees who should have been more wary of their birth families, or the way my mother had once said, *You're* our *daughter, no one else's!* in a joke attempt that struck me, even at the time, as strange and a little desperate. I couldn't have said why their possessiveness bothered me, but in retrospect I can see that it both slammed the door on my birth mother's one attempt at contact and made me feel rather like an object to be hoarded—cherished, certainly, but still a kind of commodity, not a person with a will and history of her own.

To my relief, my parents accepted my medical excuse for searching and left it at that—and so, for the time being, did I. Looking back I don't see how they could possibly have objected, given that I was pregnant with their grandchild and citing the most practical reason to search. And it was so easy for us *not* to talk about it, both because my birth parents had long been an awkward if not quite off-limits subject between us, and because all my own parents really wanted to talk about during my pregnancy was the pregnancy itself. How was I feeling? Had we gotten a crib yet? What we were going to name the baby? I answered these questions cheerfully, eager to keep their focus on their grandchild—and so this excitement dominated our every conversation, keeping them happy and distracting us all from questions about my other family.

Now that I was well beyond my first trimester and capable of doing more than plowing through my work day, eating fruit popsicles and saltines with unsalted tops, and falling asleep to *Murder, She Wrote* reruns on the couch at eight p.m., I knew it was time to shift to information-gathering mode—but anxiety about labor and delivery held me back.

While Dan checked out and read nine different pregnancy guides from the library, I created a baby registry, renewed my first aid/CPR certification, and obsessed over whether I was eating enough protein. It was not until we signed up for a birthing information session at our nearest hospital that I finally squared up to the disturbing fact that I had very little idea what labor involved, yet was—unfairly!—the one expected to go through it. And not just go through it, but make a "birth plan" and direct the entire operation. I had a general idea of the size of my cervix and the size of a newborn's head, so I was particularly keen to find out how women in the throes of labor and childbirth coped with pain. (Thus far, the most painful experience of my life had been the couple of days following my tonsillectomy in third grade.) But instead of explaining what we could expect during labor or offering suggestions on how to manage it, the hospital staff merely went over the check-in process, recited how many babies were delivered at the hospital last year, and gave us a tour of the hospital's state-of-the-art birthing suite—adding that we would be confined to the bed during labor, and therefore unable to walk around the birthing suite.

On the drive home, feeling foolish and stress-eating a granola bar I had brought along in my purse (pregnancy having taught me, if nothing else, that I should never be without snacks), I could not stop asking myself why I had ever believed I was ready to have children. *I can't do this*, I thought, *I can't. I will panic, I will seize up, I will be ripped apart.*

If being adopted had made my longing for biological family especially strong, in my mind it also made me uniquely ill-prepared for childbirth. I'd done my best to suppress my fears, because I *did* want to have children. I knew it was theoretically *possible* to carry and birth a child. But I still found it impossible to imagine, and that hardly seemed a good sign. For weeks, too, I had been consumed with the adoption search and just trying not to throw up in public, *please.* Now I was staring down my second and third trimesters with a disappearing waistline to prove it, and I still didn't know what the birth would be like. I was already a failure as a mother, and I hadn't even really begun.

What I needed now were solid facts, clear instructions. I had always found comfort in the known, in things I could control. But I couldn't ask the person I most wanted to talk to about all of this: my own mother had never given birth. And as for the one who had—bearing a baby who was too small and fragile, like I had been, was one of my greatest fears in all this. I felt the powerful and utterly foreign desire for someone, anyone, to tell me what to *do.*

Dan understood that I would feel better once I had facts and a real plan, as well as some illusion of control over the uncontrollable. He told me he would find "a *real* birth class." True to his word, he signed us up for a class with a natural childbirth instructor, starting in October. "She said the class will cover the stages of labor, pain-management techniques, pregnancy exercises, diet, and nutrition." As he said this, I felt a stir of hope that could also have been heartburn. "*And* there's a workbook."

When we arrived at the home of our childbirth instructor, Brenda, she was arranging candles in an earthen vessel filled with sand. Brenda's son, who had shown us into the room, cleared his throat to get his mother's attention, then retreated with the quick step of a middle-school-aged boy in the same room as a gigantic poster of a uterus. "Welcome," Brenda said, smiling warmly at us. "Please take a seat. Try and sit with your legs crossed, tailor-style—it strengthens your pelvic floor muscles and opens up your birth canal."

I glanced at Dan. I think we had both expected an icebreaker, some getting-to-know-you chitchat, before we began casually throwing around terms like *pelvic floor*. Even my gynecologist, not the world's chattiest health-care provider, would typically ask how I was feeling and make some sort of general comment about the weather before pulling out the stirrups. After a quick, wordless conversation, Dan and I chose two seats and watched as Brenda began lighting her candles.

As a kid in Oregon I'd sometimes visited the pungent health-food store with my mother, but I had never thought of myself as a crunchy person. While Mom was forever extolling the benefits of various herbs and vitamins, going so far as to mail me plastic bottles full of supplements intended to "boost" this or "replenish" that, I preferred to attack unpleasant symptoms with strong prescriptions. "Time to bring out the big guns, Doctor," I had been known to say. "What kind of drugs can we throw at this cough?" Enduring labor with less pain medication than I might take for a bad headache was not, for me, a particular point of pride. But I was floundering, and I needed solid information; someone who would take me by the hand and say, *This is what will happen. You will be okay.* And if that person could not be my own mother, perhaps Brenda would do.

Brenda lit the final candle she had pressed into the sand—a long white taper in the center, surrounded by smaller votives. "These are my birth candles," she explained, setting the dish on the hearth. "One of my students just called to tell me that she's in labor. Whenever I get a labor call, I light the birth candles and keep them burning until I hear that the baby has been born. Would either of you like some red raspberry leaf tea? It helps tone and strengthen your uterus."

I politely declined. "Maybe just some water, thanks," said Dan.

Additional couples began to arrive. After we introduced ourselves, Brenda handed out the promised workbooks and Dan opened at once to the first page. *What to expect in early-stage labor.* "See the pictures of the cervix, beginning to dilate and become effaced?" she asked, as if we could miss them.

One of the other students asked Brenda about her own births. "With my first child, first-stage labor lasted about twelve hours, and that felt right to me," she said. "With my second, it went so quickly that I had almost no time between contractions. I didn't get to finish my birth art."

Dan dutifully scribbled notes as Brenda talked about early labor, and I was suddenly reminded of the one and only class we'd ever taken together, months before we started dating—a philosophy course taught by a professor who managed to be sarcastic and deathly dull at the same time. After a couple of weeks, I skipped most lectures out of pure disgust, while Dan, a biomedical engineering major who didn't even need the class, went to every lecture except for one on a particularly gorgeous spring afternoon when I convinced him to play hooky and sit out on the quad with me. I did keep up with the reading, and I think in the end we both got A's, but Dan probably learned a lot more than I did. The problem, of course, was that now he could neither prepare for nor give birth for me, and I doubted that any amount of grudging independent reading or last-minute cramming would help me once labor started.

Brenda began to demonstrate various labor positions, inviting us to try them with her, and I followed accordingly. Dan had to rub my back, and all I really had to do was arrange my limbs a certain way and then breathe. It wasn't so bad. "It's important for moms to stay as relaxed as possible during contractions, and practice good abdominal breathing. Coaches!" Brenda called—this was how she addressed the partners in our class—"while Mom is breathing and relaxing, you can massage her back or shoulders or feet, help her release some tension. You should also encourage her in a low, soothing voice. Tell her she's doing a good job."

"You're doing a good job," Dan said, applying more pressure to my lower back.

Toward the end of the class, we watched a clip from a birth video, during which I learned that there are camera angles and then there are *camera angles*. My scientist husband was, of course, entirely unfazed. I didn't close my eyes, but at several points, I fixed my gaze on a point just slightly down and to the right of the television screen, hoping no one would notice I wasn't actually looking. Once the video was over, Brenda gave us "homework": many Kegel exercises for those of us who were pregnant; and, for all the couples, at least ten minutes of relaxation techniques a day ("with good abdominal breathing, remember!") in our favorite labor positions.

"There are two very important things I want you to keep in mind in the coming weeks," she said. "The first is that birth is very difficult work. There's a reason they call it *labor*. But while it may be challenging, maybe even the hardest thing you have ever done, I want you to remember that *you can do it*. Your body already knows what to do."

I closed my eyes, held on to these words, and tried to believe in them. No more thinking about bad surprises, labor horror stories, or the fact that I had surprised my own birth parents by arriving early, I vowed. No more obsessing over whether our baby would be born too early, too. Instead I called up a recent golden memory: going for a walk on the beach at sundown during a recent trip to the coast, the weekend after we found out we were having a girl. A wave had smacked into my rounded belly as I waded waist-deep in the surf, and I felt her kick—the hardest she ever had before. When I gasped a second later and then began to laugh, it wasn't because of the shock or the cold, but because her enormous kick had felt like a joyful greeting. It was *her*. Dan and I had kept our hands pressed to my stomach for hours after, feeling our child turn tiny somersaults.

Now she moved all the time, never letting me forget her for a moment. Again, I tried to imagine what she would look like. How much she might resemble me, when no one else ever had before.

Did every person giving birth feel as anxious as I did about the physical reality of pregnancy, or did my adopted experience heighten my feelings of fear and inadequacy? As eager as I was to become a parent, I had always been frightened by the sheer force and power of birth. I had very little idea what would happen to me—my mind and my heart, as well as my body—when our child made her way into the world. But I wanted to believe that our instructor was right about my body knowing what to do. I wanted to have that kind of faith in myself.

As Dan and I walked to our car after class, I resisted the urge to make a joke about how terrible my birth art and birth poems were going to be. There was a lot I could have highlighted about the strange newness of natural childbirth class, the fear I still harbored about a pain I could not imagine, the doubts I had about what kind of parent I would be. But I could not deny that I felt less anxious than I had in weeks.

Maybe my intermediary would find my birth family, maybe she wouldn't—but this life about to begin was its own expanding universe of promise and possibility. One way or another, my family—the one *I* had chosen to create—was growing. Our child's birth might prove empowering for me, not simply terrifying, for all its mystery and all my fear.

I felt suddenly, deeply grateful for Brenda, for her posters and her workbook, for her brace of birth candles shining through the night. She had helped me view birth as something to be understood and cooperated with, something *I* could do, however unnatural and unknown my own birth story was. In the weeks to come, I would draw so much knowledge and comfort from her class. I would think about her words, her quiet confidence in us, when labor finally began on a chilly midwinter night.

Dan and I drove home, talking about baby names and nursery paint colors and the crib we still had to purchase. All the time, Brenda's promise—my new pregnancy mantra—rolled through my mind. *You can do this,* I told myself. *You can.*

W hile my thoughts often strayed to my birth family and how Donna's search might be going, the baby was foremost in my mind as I neared the end of the second trimester. One evening in early November, I assigned myself the pleasant job of folding and putting away freshly laundered onesies and footed pajamas in what was to be her room. The small space had recently undergone a transformation from office to nursery, its walls now a cheerful violet, a white wooden crib in one corner and a changing table in another. As I buttoned snaps and smoothed edges on her tiny outfits, I realized that every stitch of clothing the baby currently owned could fit into a single dresser drawer. For someone who would change our lives, she would take up so little space.

When my phone rang, I glanced down and saw a 206 area code. Seattle. My knees seemed to disappear for the briefest of moments as I fumbled to accept the call, heart already thundering. I knew it wouldn't be *them*, of course. It was Donna. Just Donna, and still, my voice shook a little as I said, "Hello?"

My intermediary didn't waste time with pleasantries. Nor did she seem especially interested in drawing out the suspense. "I found your birth family, Nicole! Your file is in my hands *right now*."

I clutched the phone tightly so I wouldn't drop it, lowering myself into the rocking chair. I knew that many of the personal details about my birth parents couldn't be shared until they had consented to further contact. Still, Donna must be able to share *some* information, or she wouldn't have called. "What can you tell me?"

She seized on the question as though she had been waiting years, not minutes, to share the news. "Not a lot, unfortunately, but what's here is very interesting! Did you know that you have sisters?"

I'd long known that I had sisters, though I had never known the precise number, or their names or ages. I tried to imagine them, again, and was unable to picture a single woman who had my eyes, or my smile, or my laugh. But they were out there, somewhere— sisters who might have been my childhood playmates, sisters who might want to meet me.

Donna told me that two sisters, a half sister and a full one, had been living at home at the time I was born. Then she added, with devastating casualness, "The social worker wrote she got the impression that your parents might have wanted a boy, not another girl."

I don't remember what I said in response. I do remember I suddenly felt like crying. Even though it was speculation, even though I had no way of knowing if it was true.

Donna said she had found a statement of divorce from 1987; my birth parents now lived in separate states. I would have been six years old at the time they divorced. How old would my sisters have been? What must that have been like for them—to lose a sister to adoption, and then watch their parents split up?

I had always imagined writing to my birth parents, talking with them, even meeting them, at the same time—never had I imagined a reunion with just one or the other. But perhaps it was not shocking, after all, that their marriage had ended. My adoption must have been enormously stressful, in addition to whatever factors had led to it; many marriages fell apart under less strain.

Citing my file, Donna confirmed other things I already knew: I was born more than two months early and spent weeks in the neonatal intensive care unit; my birth parents had been given the doctors' grim prognoses. It was a relief, in a way, to hear the old information repeated, echoes of the history I'd always known. A respite from surprises, before another shock.

"The social worker thought your birth parents might be worried about what people in their community might think if they brought home a sick baby," she said. "They also didn't want to have to explain why you didn't come home at all. They thought it would be easier if they told everyone, including your sisters, that you had died at birth."

Her voice ran ahead, but I no longer wanted to try to keep up. I couldn't seem to speak, to interrupt or shout at her to stop like I wanted to—I was frozen, staring blankly at the crib and the onesies and the purple-hued quilt my mother-in-law had sewn for the baby. This was worse than hearing about my birth parents' divorce, worse than wondering if they would have preferred a boy to "another girl." Had I been easier to give up because I hadn't been healthy? Had they really spent the years since the adoption denying my existence to everyone—even my own sisters? If so, what kind of people did that make them?

Had they ever wanted me at all?

I don't know how long it was before I realized Donna was still talking. I heard her asking me if I was "thrilled" to be this close to finding my birth parents. She thought this was *good* news, I realized; she had been waiting for weeks to retrieve my file and now she was able to reveal all the poignant details. Was I going to write to them? she wanted to know. What was the next step?

Years earlier, when a friend asked if I idealized my birth parents, if I envisioned them as paragons whose absence from my life made them only too easy to imagine and to love, I had scoffed at the question. *Of course I know they aren't perfect!* But deep down, I knew that I had cast them as courageous people who made a difficult decision out of love, as many birth parents do. Every snippet of information, every crumb for which I had begged, every tale I'd been told at my mother's knee bolstered this vision of my biological parents as strong, selfless people who had sacrificed the chance to know and raise me so I could have a better life. It was the story I'd had to believe in, the one I'd treasured because it meant I had been loved.

On the other end of the line, Donna's voice finally, mercifully slowed. I knew I had to say something, tell her what I wanted to do, but I had no idea. I felt drained of excitement, of curiosity, even of questions. If I opened my eyes to find my birth parents standing right in front of me, I wouldn't have known what to say. Who knew what I'd find in pursuit of the truth? Would my child, my husband, thank me for bringing these new relatives into our lives? I had been so sure about my decision to look for them—so sure that I was doing the right thing, for my baby and for myself. What was worse, to know nothing? Or to learn things that broke my heart?

I didn't *have* to write to them. I could just leave them alone. I could be content, leave everything as it was, and maybe—with my new family, with Dan and this baby I loved so much—maybe that would be enough.

Into the silence, Donna spoke again. "There's just one more thing you might like to know . . ." I heard paper rustling in the background. "There's a name here in the file. I guess your parents chose it for you before you were adopted."

I felt my heart, which had sunk, begin to thump hard again. A name? One they'd given me? "What was it?"

"Susan."

Susan. Such a pretty, old-fashioned name. I spun through recollections of all the Susans I had ever known: My beloved second-grade teacher. An old friend of the family. A girl who had lived in my dorm in college. I almost laughed: I didn't *look* like a Susan.

I'd always assumed my birth parents hadn't bothered to give me a name. I'd been in their lives for a few days only, maybe a few hours. If I were giving up the right to raise my child—if I knew I might never see her again—would I still want to give her a name? Would it help, somehow, to remember her by that name, even if I knew she wasn't going to keep it?

The name wasn't much to go on. It wasn't proof of their love for me. It told me nothing about who they were, what they valued, if they had wanted me. But it was enough to nudge me back onto the path I had chosen months ago—the one I still wanted to follow, though I was less certain than ever about what I would find.

I didn't think my parents would have named a child they cared nothing about.

"I'll work on the letter," I said. What I didn't say, but thought: *I will be brave. I will see this through.*

As soon as I heard the name my birth parents chose for me, I'd made my choice. Again I thought of my own daughter, not yet born but very much wanted. When the call was over, I left her future room and went in search of my laptop, pulling up one of the many baby-name sites Dan and I had been consulting. *Abigail*, I already knew, meant "my father's joy." *Julia* meant "youthful."

A new search told me that *Susan* meant "lily." What had the name meant to my birth parents? Why had they chosen it?

Someday soon, perhaps, I might know.

D onna instructed me to write two separate letters, one for each of my birth parents. I shouldn't include too many details. I shouldn't mention where I grew up or where I went to school. I shouldn't sign my last name. I shouldn't share any "identifying" or personal information until they agreed to be in contact.

I decided to focus on one reunion at a time. I would write to my birth mother first, hear what she had to say—if she chose to reply— and then write to my birth father.

Ever since my phone conversation with Donna, my birth parents seemed more complicated, more human. More real. Somewhere out there, my birth mother was living her life; I didn't know exactly where. Did she live alone? With one of my siblings? Was she in a little city apartment or a sprawling suburban home? Did she still go to work, or was she now, in her sixties, retired?

Whenever I pictured her, moving through her days with no premonition of my plans, I nearly lost my nerve. I knew she might be perfectly content with the way things were, no longer curious about me. Yet I also knew there was a time when *she* had been the one to reach out. In the years since she had sent that letter to my adoptive parents, had she stopped thinking of me? My letter to her would change both our lives, just as her choice to give me up had, and there was no way to ask permission; to warn her that the child she'd given away—perhaps, by now, given up on—was only a letter away.

Donna emailed to ask about the letter, as if I needed reminding. But I would not be rushed. These were the first words my mother would ever read from me, and they had to be *right*. They had to be perfect.

Two weeks before Christmas, a month after I'd learned I had once been called *Susan*, I sat down with my laptop and opened a new file, ignoring the half dozen drafts I had already started. I vowed not to rise until I had finished the letter.

Dear Mom

I couldn't erase that greeting fast enough. It still felt wrong to refer to another woman as *Mom*, and I shouldn't claim my birth mother as family when I had no idea how she thought of me. But the opening was a dilemma: I didn't know her last name, or whether she went by Ms. or Mrs.

Hello, my name is Nicole. I am your biological daughter—born on May 5, 1981, and placed for adoption in July 1981. You are probably wondering why I'm contacting you now. I know this letter is bound to come as a shock to you. Still, I hope it's not an unhappy one.

I now confronted the problem of deciding exactly what to tell her. I had been instructed not to share any personal details. But I had to offer *something*. If I had a daughter I had never known and had the chance to learn something about her, what would matter most to me?

I want you to know that I am well, and happy, and have lived a good life. I was raised by parents who loved me very much.

On the solid ground of my adoptive family's love, I began to feel more secure in my words. In many ways, I had been lucky. I had been loved. These were all facts I thought my birth mother would care about, facts she deserved to know. But did it sound like I believed *she* didn't love me? I typed faster, reaching for reassurances.

I know that the adoption decision could not have been an easy one for you. I have always respected you for making what you believed was the best choice for me. I hope it brings you some peace and reassurance to know what a good life I've had. I'm writing to you now because I would like to know a little bit more about your family, if you are willing to share.

The letter marching line by line down the page was no work of art. It was vague, as it had to be, free from the questions I had waited nearly twenty-seven years to ask. I still needed her permission before I could turn to all of those.

But, I realized, I did have something I wanted to say.

If I could only say one thing to you, it would just be this: thank you. You made a very difficult decision 27 years ago—you gave up the chance to know and raise me so that I could be cared for by someone else.

It was wrenching to think about my adoptive parents while writing a letter to my birth mother.

"*Now?* Haven't you got enough going on with the baby?" my mom said, when I finally told her I was going to write to my birth family myself.

"I'm doing this *because* I'm having a baby," I said. That much was true. But in a moment of compassion or cowardice—perhaps both?—I appealed again to my mother's practical nature; to the woman who had worked in hospitals for years and had always known I was coming down with something before I noticed myself. "I told you I wanted my medical history," I reminded her. "This is the only way I'll get it. I never found out why my birth mother had me so early. I don't know what diseases run in my family. I'm getting older, starting my own family . . . I need this information."

Mom agreed that my medical history was important. Again, for the good of her grandchild. What else could she say? She said it was too bad I could only get it by writing to them. "Will you talk with them, too?"

"Yes," I said. "If they want to talk to me."

She told me not to forget who my real family was. As if I could forget—they were the only family I'd ever known. We all knew what I owed them; it went without saying: I would not call another parent *Mom* or *Dad*. I would not replace my adoptive family with my biological one.

Yet my biological family was the one I'd been made for. Whoever they were, my birth parents were the people who had brought me into the world, and I wanted them to know I recognized that; I could honor them for it, even if I never learned anything else about them. I felt I owed *them* that much.

I've had a full, healthy, happy life. And I have you to thank for that life.

I tried to put myself in my birth mother's place. As I couldn't conjure a clear image of her face, I settled for picturing her hands—like mine, perhaps, but smaller, lined with age. I saw them opening the mailbox, retrieving my letter, unfolding the two sheets of paper. How would she react when she realized the words were mine? Would she weep from joy or sadness? Would she resent the sudden intrusion into her life?

If you would like to write back to me, the person forwarding this letter to you can share my information. If you would rather not

*write or call, then please consider sending the medical and family
history back to me. Whatever you choose, thank you for reading
this letter.*

"Best wishes" seemed impersonal; "Sincerely" was worse. I hesitated. Then I typed:

*Love,
Nicole*

If not something I felt, not precisely, not yet, love was something I aspired to. She was my mother, or she had been at one time. Maybe a part of me just wanted to love the idea of her.

In the end, I wasn't entirely satisfied with my letter. There was so much I couldn't ask, yet so much I had to pack into a handful of paragraphs. I wanted my words to be warm, clever, reassuring, but instead I'd essentially written a note of introduction, sprinkled with assurances of my well-being and hints about my life that didn't give too much away. That was how we had to begin, Donna had said; everything else—if there was to be anything else—would have to wait.

The week before Christmas, I finally printed out the letter, signed it by hand, and mailed it off, resisting the urge to tear it apart word by word and make it anew. My birth mother wouldn't make the decision to talk with me based on my wit or my word choices.

Donna emailed to let me know she had received it, adding that there was "an unwritten law" among intermediaries not to reach out to biological relatives close to the holidays. *It's a very emotional time for people. They tend to have too much stress at holiday time.* She said she would mail it after Christmas—definitely before New Year's.

On New Year's Day, I would begin my thirty-second week of pregnancy. My birth mother had never reached that point with me.

While I'd hoped to be in touch with my birth family by the time I delivered my daughter, now my task was simply to hold and wait for the choices of others to determine what happened next. With the letter written and sent at last, the uncertainty was somehow easier to bear. Everything in my life was about to change; I would savor the peace, the calm, while I still could.

A few days into the new year, Cindy was at the community health clinic where she worked. She was not a doctor, or a nurse, but the person who kept things running: she managed schedules for the director of the clinic as well as multiple staff, always knew who was supposed to be on call, and was the one who had an answer when no one else knew what was going on. She liked her work; she knew her value, and was always busy.

So when she got a cryptic email from Jessica—*Call me right away*—she ignored it at first. She had a lot to do; she could check in with Jessica when the workday was over. Cindy assumed she wanted to talk about their mother, who had moved in with Jessica in another state. But then came a string of increasingly urgent texts (*Are you there? It's really important*), so Cindy slipped out to make the call. "Hey. What's going on?"

She listened, mostly, while Jessica talked at high speed. Even if there had been an opportunity to interrupt, ask more questions, Cindy had no idea what to say. Their family had its problems; their parents had their secrets, no doubt. But what Jessica was telling her seemed too outrageous. Even for them. It couldn't possibly be true.

Could it?

Cindy heard herself telling Jessica that her break was over; she had to get back to work. But she didn't. Instead she walked over to her coworker's desk. Her friend took one look at Cindy's face and asked what had happened.

"I just found out that I have a sister," Cindy told her. "I thought she was dead ... but she's not. She was adopted."

Her coworker was the mother of two children, both adopted from foster care. She gently took Cindy by the arm. "Come on," she said, and led her toward the door. "We're going for a walk."

That evening, when they both got home from work, Cindy told her husband, Rick, what she had learned. She had met Rick in the army reserves and married him in 2002. He was one of few people she'd ever told about what her childhood was like.

"They *lied* to us," she said over and over.

That her parents had withheld information, that they had secrets beyond her ability to imagine, was not so shocking. But *why* had they covered it up? That was the part Cindy couldn't understand. They had always insisted they didn't have to explain anything to her. *That's our business, not yours.* They could have told her the truth about the adoption, forbidden any further discussion, and that would have been that. She would never have gotten anything else out of them, but at least she would have known. Instead they had managed to hide a sister—"a whole *person*!"—from her.

The baby had been a girl, she remembered that much. They were going to call her Susie. She'd long since forgotten nearly everything else about that strange, confusing time when she was almost a big sister, but Cindy distinctly remembered that name, the name they had chosen.

For an instant, Rick was speechless; uncharacteristically so. Then he remembered when Cindy began to tell him about her family, back when they were newly dating. It had taken time to explain it all—the story came out painstakingly over many long drives and weekend trips—and that was how Rick came to understand the kind of pressure she'd lived under when she was young. Maybe that's what he was remembering when he admitted that, while the adoption was a wild story, he could believe it.

"Get as much information as you can," he said. "Then you can figure out what you want to do."

So Cindy got Jessica on the phone again. She learned that a young woman had sent their mother a letter through an adoption intermediary. She had asked for medical information. She was having a baby soon. She had grown up in Oregon. *So close*, Cindy thought. For all those years, her sister had been so close.

Their mother's English had never been strong. Her daughters had often helped her decipher bills and contracts and other important documents. When the mysterious letter had arrived, she was confused by it; she couldn't understand. So she'd asked Jessica to help translate.

That was how Jessica learned that their sister was still alive.

Their mother didn't try to deny it; yes, she said, it was true. The girl had been tiny, and sick, but she had lived. She had been adopted by another family. "Mom said they couldn't afford the medical bills," Jessica said. "*He* said that adoption was the only choice."

Their mother told Jessica the adoption was her husband's "fault"; that she herself had wanted to tell the daughters the truth about their sister, but he wouldn't allow it. They wondered if this was true. They remembered once, years ago, before she died, their grandmother had mentioned something about *your other sister*. Had she been confused in her old age, or had she known about the adoption that was hidden from them?

Jessica didn't know if the young woman had also reached out to Cindy's father. During the years they'd all been together, Cindy's father, though not Jessica's biological parent, had been a father to both of them. But after the divorce, Jessica had stayed in touch only with their mother, and when Cindy went to live with her father the two sisters weren't permitted to communicate. They tried to keep in touch across the miles, but rarely saw each other. Now Cindy no longer talked to their mother, and Jessica was not in contact with Cindy's father; they knew they would have to get the story out of each parent, separately, and compare notes.

They couldn't move forward with their sister until the proper forms were signed and filed, and it would take some time—maybe a few weeks, maybe a month. Jessica promised to pass along her contact information as soon as she could. "But let's not tell her about the bad things, Cindy," she added. "Let's keep it positive. Once she knows us better, maybe we could tell her more of what happened. We don't want to scare her away, do we?"

Cindy could see the logic in this. She didn't want to scare her sister away, either. But all her life, she had been told what to say and what not to say. She'd been subject to them all, to their values and their rules: *Don't tell anyone about what happens at home. Don't tell anyone about the divorce. Keep the family secrets; help us save face.* And she had gone along with it, if sometimes grudgingly, even when it meant that terrible things went unspoken, unacknowledged. As the youngest, she had known her opinion counted least, counted last—if at all.

But this, she couldn't help but feel, was different. Already she felt a surge of resentment at being told how to handle this revelation, what to say when she made contact. She wasn't a child anymore. And who was she to try to keep secrets from this girl who'd been given up, whose very existence had been denied?

Cindy was two weeks away from turning thirty-three when she learned that her family was not what she'd always believed. Her little sister was alive. She had been raised by strangers. What had they been like, her little sister's parents? How might her sister's childhood compare with hers? Had she been safe? Had she been happy?

Cindy would write to her as soon as she could, she knew that already. She just had to decide what to tell her.

I felt as though I'd been staring at a waiting chessboard all my life, and now the dusty old pieces were finally beginning to move. A few days into January, Donna called to tell me that my birth mother had received my letter, and that one of my sisters had helped her to read it. I fully intended to ask more about my birth mother, to find out if she was eager to talk to me, but was momentarily distracted—what about my sisters? Donna couldn't share their full names, but my half sister was named Jessica, and my full sister, Cindy.

Donna couldn't send me my birth family's contact information, or share mine. It would take a few weeks to collect and file the paperwork. In the meantime, if I wanted to, I could prepare another letter for my birth father, and Donna would forward it to him. "I know waiting is hard," she said. She was right, but it was even harder to try to wrest emotional focus away from the baby as I drew nearer to full term. I confirmed that Donna could tell me nothing new and said goodbye.

How strange that the weeks of my pregnancy had been spent waiting, looking ahead, not just to the birth but also to my hoped-for reunion with my family of origin. While I had thought of my pregnancy and my search as parallel journeys, I had not expected the two winding paths to join together here, now, at the summit. The slow-turning cogs of bureaucracy and my own hesitancy in composing the letter to my birth mother forced this pair of stories to converge: I might rejoin one family while beginning another. Would it all be too much for me to handle? Even if it was, what choice did I have, except to move forward?

Only after I'd hung up did I realize that I'd forgotten to ask Donna if she could tell me my birth mother's name.

One week into February—an email from Jessica. *Hello, Nicole. I am not sure how to start or what to say. It was never clear to me what happened 26 years ago. Our parents told us you had died.*

I felt sad and angry again when I read those words, though I wasn't sure I had a right to either feeling. It hurt to see a guess from my adoption file confirmed in black-and-white on my computer screen: my birth parents had never told their other children about me. They let them believe I had died in the hospital.

I couldn't help but feel guilty for what my sisters must have gone through. They might be eager to speak, as my intermediary had put it, but that didn't mean they hadn't been shaken by their parents' omission. And I—with my curiosity, my determined pursuit of the facts, my selfishness?—was the reason. I had questions, yes, and I had much to gain from a search. But did I truly have the right to disrupt my sisters' lives with a letter announcing a truth their parents had not wanted to reveal? In time, as everyone learned more about what happened, would they come to resent the stranger who had shattered the family equilibrium? Perhaps they blamed me already.

But Jessica did not seem to believe I was at fault. She told me that she had read my letter, seen the enclosed photographs, and confronted our mother, who had told her about the adoption. They had been struggling financially, Jessica said, and they could not afford the medical bills. My birth father, Jessica was told, had suggested that adoption was "the best way." I paused at these words, a direct echo of the story I'd heard time and time again from my adoptive parents.

Jessica said that our mother would prefer to talk with me on the phone. *When you are ready*, she added. In the meantime, they would fill out the medical forms and send them back via the intermediary. *This is all meant to be*, she wrote, *with God's help.* The invocation reminded me of my adoptive parents, who'd been so convinced that God had willed my adoption—others still seemed to see divine planning, the hand of fate, where I saw the result of every small, careful step I had been weighing over the course of months; years.

Jessica told me that she thought our mother must have kept a great deal of pain inside, and now, she was implying, I could help her heal. I had trouble thinking so highly of my healing abilities. That my birth parents had kept my adoption hidden seemed to me an ominous sign, proof that they had never been at peace with the decision. I felt so foolish for having once imagined them explaining it to my siblings, telling them: *It was a difficult decision, but it was the right one.* Even if they hadn't wanted to tell them as children, I'd reasoned, surely they could have sat them down at some point, as adults, and given them the truth. But they never had.

What should I do now? I didn't see how talking with me once, or even many times, would help my birth mother feel better about a choice she'd buried so deep her own children had not known about it. Nothing I had learned so far made me eager to book a flight to the west coast to meet everyone.

Contact had always been a risk. I had pursued it because I felt it was important; because I knew not everything in life could remain simple and compartmentalized forever. But as I thought about how to respond, I realized I had no idea what would happen next. They had all learned far more about me than I knew about them. If they didn't even share their truths with one another, what could *I* hope to learn?

There is another sister. Her name is Cindy. She is 33 years old, and beautiful like you. I told her about you.

This was the part of Jessica's email that interested me more than all the rest. I read these words over and over, trying to think what "beautiful like me" could mean—I'd never thought of myself as attractive, partly a function of growing up in my overwhelmingly white hometown. As my full sister, did Cindy look the most like me out of all of them? Was she taller or shorter than me? Was she also a night owl, chatty but socially awkward, too lazy for makeup, always in the middle of reading five books at once? Did she save her best singing for the car? Did she ever dream about becoming a writer?

Where my birth parents were concerned, I now felt an urge, justified or not, to protect myself—not to shut things down, but to proceed slowly and warily, for reasons I could not quite identify. But despite these misgivings and the guilt I felt over my sisters' shock, knowing that they were no longer in ignorance of my existence filled me with a strange hope, a wild and new kind of happiness.

They were out there. They might want to know more about me. Whatever had happened with our parents, whatever might have gone wrong in our family, maybe this was a new beginning.

Cindy knew she had to give her father a chance to explain. She couldn't simply drive the three and a half hours to his house uninvited, not in the middle of the workweek. So she called him the day after she learned the truth from Jessica.

"I have to ask you something," she said. "Do I have a sister you never told me about?"

There was a long pause. "Do you mean your half sister?"

"No." She could already feel her anger rising. "Another sister, my full sister. Did you and Mom ever have a baby you didn't tell us about?"

The denial was immediate, but his voice sounded a bit strange. He said he didn't know if her mother had had another baby with someone after the divorce, but there were no other children he knew about. "If there had been another child, don't you think you'd already know?" he asked.

Cindy thought of her sister's letter. It was too much, too detailed to be a fabrication. Somewhere, there were documents, birth and adoption decrees: hard proof, even if she hadn't seen it yet. And Cindy knew the letter had included photos. Jessica had told her there was a family resemblance.

She *knew* that she had a sister. She had known for a matter of days. Her father had known for almost twenty-seven years. She didn't know what she expected when she called, but she had hoped he would admit it. Tell her why her sister had been given away.

But if she felt confused, disappointed, she was also resigned. All her life, it had been drilled into her not to talk back, not to get upset, not to question her family. She had other means of getting the story now. If her father didn't want to tell her what had happened, Cindy didn't have the will or the energy to try to change his mind. Not tonight. "Okay," she said, and ended the call.

Cindy and Rick—whose birthdays were in January, days apart—had been planning to spend their birthday weekend with her father and stepmother. Now Cindy couldn't imagine going ahead with the visit as planned. There was no way she was going to see them, she told Rick. She signed up to be on call at the clinic that weekend, which effectively made it impossible for her to travel, and then called and told her stepmom that she and Rick were staying home.

Her stepmother was not only disappointed, but troubled: Cindy's father had been acting strangely ever since their call. He seemed anxious. He had been queasy. Now Cindy and Rick weren't coming to visit? What was wrong with everyone? What was going on?

Cindy loved her stepmother. In many ways, she had been more of a parent to her than anyone else; she had helped give Cindy the only stable home she'd known as a child. Her father would most likely prefer she not say anything about the adoption to her stepmom. But Cindy didn't want to lie to the woman who'd raised her, and she couldn't bring herself to deny how upset she was.

She was so tired of the lies.

"I just found out I have a sister no one ever told me about," she said.

"*What?* What do you mean? Who is she?"

"She's my full sister. She sent a letter to our mom. They had her when I was six years old. When I asked Dad, he said he didn't know anything about it."

"I see," her stepmother said. "Well, we certainly have a lot to talk about. We'll come to your house."

Cindy didn't think that was a good idea. She didn't feel ready to confront her father. But her stepmom insisted they were coming that very weekend.

Maybe, Cindy thought, her father would tell her more in person. She agreed to the visit, instructing her concerned husband to "behave" while her parents were there. Then she steeled herself for the hardest conversation she would ever have with her father.

I n the first picture Cindy ever sent me, she is smiling
so you can't see her teeth, dark brown eyes gazing directly into the camera. Her shoulder-length
black hair is pulled back in what I now know to be her customary
ponytail. A white top and a long brown skirt skim her slender, sturdy
frame. She and her husband, Rick, are standing in front of some trees
in someone's backyard, and my sister's face and arms look paler than
usual in the sunlight. You cannot see her freckles.

*Nicole, I was very shocked to find out I had another sister. I don't
know how much you want to know. Our parents told us that you
died. I have heard two versions of the story since we found out
about you, and it could be both are untrue or only one is true.*

There she was, my sister. I don't know how long I stared at the
picture, eagerly searching for the familiar in her face. "I always expected your sisters to look like you, only a little older," Dan said.
"You two really do look very different." But, he added, Cindy was
my closest genetic relative, and though we'd never pass for twins, the
resemblance was undeniable.

I could see we were alike, but it was difficult to name just *how* we were alike. As I homed in on her features, I cataloged, one by one, the disparities between our eyes and our noses, the shapes of our faces, the sweep of our hair. The differences were easy to spot; they announced themselves. There was no single thing I could point to and say, *That's me.* Yet as Dan had pointed out, no one who saw us together would doubt we were sisters.

I thought of my years in Oregon, my white school and our white neighborhood, all the times I'd wished I could just talk to someone who looked like me. My longing for Korean family, for people who understood, was one of so many things my adoptive parents had not been told to expect; the day I came home from school and told her how much I wished I knew other Asians stuck in my mother's memory precisely because it had surprised her. I didn't mention the bullies, but I didn't have to—as someone who loved me, she felt uneasy just knowing that I had noticed. Eventually, I had learned to stop voicing such thoughts. What could my parents say about it? What could they do?

I sent my own pictures to Cindy, the same ones I had included in the letter to our mother: a black-and-white photo of Dan and me on our wedding day, and a picture of me sitting alone in our woodsy backyard in our woodsy backyard. She told me that she loved the photos, and thanked me for sending them. *I keep looking at your face, and I think you look a little like both Mom and Dad.*

Cindy said she was trying to gather information. She was no longer in touch with our mother, but she had heard her side of it from Jessica, and was also talking with our father. During a recent visit, our father told Cindy he had believed it would be too terrible for her, knowing that she had a sister who had been given away. He had been sure she would go to a good family, a good home. *Knowing how our family was,* Cindy wrote to me, *I have to agree the adoption was probably for the best.*

I thought of all the times I had heard that phrase—*for the best*—

or one like it. I was sure my sister believed it was true, and perhaps it was in my case. But I was growing so tired of it, this line we all said to try to make something simple out of a deeply complicated situation. It was no longer enough.

All the same, there was an openness in Cindy's emails that immediately appealed to me—maybe I took it as an early hint that we were alike, at least, in how our minds worked, or in valuing the truth. Maybe the barely leashed anger I sensed beneath her compassionate words also came as a kind of reassurance, proof that something important had happened. We were united, even if it was only in our curiosity and frustration at a lack of openness in our family. She clearly didn't blame me for unwittingly revealing such an enormous family secret. But she also felt wronged, and made it clear she would accept nothing but the truth going forward.

She said she had asked our father if he would like to be in touch with me. I still hadn't written to him. After learning they'd hidden the adoption, I had wondered if he would even want to hear from me—I'd almost convinced myself that he wouldn't. Our mother had told Jessica that he hadn't wanted me, and that was partly why he pushed for the adoption. It didn't make me eager to reach out. But Cindy believed he felt differently.

I spoke to my father last month and he expressed guilt and shame for having made the decision to give you away. He is interested in speaking with you if you wish to speak to him.

Cindy seemed to want to know everything—everything she hadn't been told. Just knowing that my sister and I might share the same questions about what had happened to our family felt like vindication decades in the making.

Nicole—Nikki—I feel very fortunate that you have let us in your life and want to know who we are.

She had used my nickname. I tried to remember: in my letter to my birth mom, I was sure I'd signed off as *Nicole*, but maybe I had mentioned that friends call me *Nikki*. Family, too. It was silly and fanciful to imagine Cindy calling me that if we'd grown up together, since I knew my birth family had planned to call me Susie. But I liked that she was already using the name chosen by the people closest to me.

I never asked Cindy to demand answers from our parents. I wouldn't have presumed, especially not so soon after connecting with her. Without my having to ask, she promised: *I will not hide anything from you that is mine to share.* There was still so much we didn't know, but at last, I wasn't all alone in my wondering.

A week after receiving Cindy's first email, I reached full term. The girl who had filled my thoughts since long before she could make herself known in kicks and rolls was big enough to be born. People kept asking how I was doing, often with a half-knowing smile and some variation on "Bet you're ready for that kid to be born!" I thought I was. But inside, she was safe, and I was safe from whatever her birth would bring, an upheaval I wasn't sure I was ready for.

As Cindy's emails flooded my inbox, the reality of reunion began to feel overwhelming. Even as I devoured my sister's words, a part of me resented my decision to search, the resulting distraction from our baby's impending birth. And on nights when I did find myself awake in the wee hours, staring up at the ceiling, mind awhirl, it was always due to some new tidbit of information about my birth family, not the discomfort of being fully nine months pregnant.

Jessica said that our mother had a hard, disappointing life; that she believed the adoption and the divorce and everything else that had gone wrong were due to her husband's decisions. Cindy said that our parents divorced because they fought all the time, and that most of their fights stemmed from the way our mother treated

Cindy. *Our family was rife with problems. There is a lot I would love to tell you. But if you want, we can live in the present and I won't mention difficult things.*

Cindy was offering me a choice: I could tell her I didn't want to know about the "difficult things," hide from new knowledge that would complicate the vision I'd had of my birth family. We could focus solely on the joy of being reunited. As Jessica said, the past was the past.

I didn't want to be disappointed. I had wanted to find my birth family for so long. But I was the one who had burst into their lives, and if I learned things that upset me, well, my relatives were only scrambling to respond to a situation *I* had created. I didn't know what to make of my birth parents, but with Cindy, at least, I didn't want to begin with lies and omissions. I didn't want her to have to hide anything she had experienced or any part of who she was. Whatever she had been through, I wanted to know—to listen to and honor it. I didn't have the inclination or energy to present a façade. What was the point of being reunited, being *sisters*, if we were both still alone?

You can tell me anything you want, I wrote to her. *I would rather know.*

It was eleven p.m. in my mother's time zone when I called her— would she even pick up?

She answered after a few rings. "Hi! Did you have the baby?"

"No, I'm still pregnant."

I was sorry to disappoint her. Of course that was what she would think when I called her in the middle of the night, my time.

"Oh. Well, what's up?"

Feeling helpless, I looked around our living room, silent and free from baby accoutrements—if not for long. When I slipped out of bed and took myself downstairs at two in the morning so my tossing and turning wouldn't wake my husband, my mother had suddenly seemed like the only person in the world to call.

I told her that I'd been talking a lot with Cindy: "Emailing, mostly." Mom didn't sound upset to hear this—on the contrary, her voice perked up considerably, despite the late hour. That was awfully exciting, wasn't it? What was Cindy like? Where did she live? What did she do for work? Did she have kids?

I wondered only a little at my mother's reaction. Sisters, after all, were safe. Sisters could never take the place of parents.

Cindy and Jessica had never known about the adoption, I explained. Each had talked to the parent of their choice, and the resulting stories conflicted. "Cindy believes her dad. She doesn't talk to her mother at all. She told me her childhood was really unhappy."

"Unhappy how?"

Cindy had told me that our mother had abused her. That she hit her, nearly every day. I opened my mouth a few times to say this, but the truth felt stuck like a hard lump in my throat. It wasn't disbelief or even disappointment causing me to choke on my words. It was shame: shame that chilled me through.

How could I be so disappointed in someone I had never even met?

My mother was still waiting. Why couldn't I tell her? Why else had I called home, if not to tell her what I had learned about the woman who bore me? Saying it aloud wasn't going to be what made it true. I already *knew* it was true; I believed my sister, even though what she told me ran counter to everything I had ever wanted to believe about my birth mother.

Earlier that day, when I'd told Dan, his shock and sorrow had been what I had expected. "I'm so sorry. I'm sorry for you and Cindy. That's so horrible." And then he'd asked the question I still did not know how to answer. "What are you going to do?" We both knew what he meant: *What are you going to do about your birth mother? Are you going to talk to her?*

"Cindy said that our mother used to beat her." I forced the words out, one by one. "Cindy was afraid of her."

One of my birth family's many secrets, maybe the biggest one.

But Cindy had said she didn't care who I told. *You're family.* Even if we didn't grow up together, she seemed to be saying, this was part of my history, too. Because she was sure that the abuse was one reason our father had suggested adoption.

Cindy got hit all the time. Like it was nothing. Like she deserved it. And for a long time, she thought this was normal. She imagined that her treatment was the lot of all youngest children. But then she had started noticing the other kids at school: how they didn't seem to be afraid all the time; how they had nice clothes and shoes that fit; how they had a packed lunch or lunch money every single day. They must have had someone at home who took care of them, she realized.

Her mother always believed she was justified in her anger, which could last for hours or days, and over which she seemed to have no control. She believed she had every right to "discipline" her own child. Cindy tried to tell a teacher what was happening, but the teacher didn't believe her. She ran away. She slept outside on a bench, or in the woods, when it was warm enough. One time the police found her, listened to her, saw her bruises, and called child protective services. She spent a few weeks in a foster home. Eventually, she was released after her parents promised the abuse would stop. It never did—until after the divorce, when she went to live with her father.

I was distantly aware that Cindy told me the truth because she was trying to protect me. She barely knew me, but she didn't want to see me hurt. *I didn't want to taint your idea of our mom,* she wrote. *But I have been wanting to tell you just so you would be cautious.*

Sitting there on my sofa talking to my mother, hugely pregnant and fighting tears, I couldn't yet understand that my birth mother's nature would become the invisible thread connecting all my anxieties, my many shortcomings, all my worst moments as a parent. That it would cause me to question my instincts, bring me up short every time I lost my temper with one of my children. Years later, I would think of her when I stopped, mid-argument, to give my tear-ful daughter permission to challenge me if she ever thought I was be-ing unfair: *You can always tell me. You can say,* I think you're being too hard on me right now, *and I promise I'll stop and listen to you.*

The hopes I'd once harbored about talking with my birth mother, getting to know her—even the simple vision of us meeting face-to-face, embracing as parent and child—seemed so foolish now. I knew that whether we ever spoke, whether we met in person, I would never be able to think of her without also thinking of my sister. Per-haps our mother *had* wanted to keep me, for reasons I might never know. But I would never again be able to think of her as someone I had been meant to stay with. I wouldn't imagine her looking at me with love on the last day she ever saw me. I'd picture her towering over my sister as a little girl, venting her anger and unhappiness on the small shoulders of a child who could not escape.

"I guess it's a good thing you didn't grow up with her," Mom said.

She didn't sound triumphant, exactly, but I still flinched. I left it alone. I hadn't called her to argue. I wasn't sure why I had called, really, or what I wanted from her—until suddenly I heard myself asking, "Do you think I could ever do something like that?"

There was a long pause. I was sure she wouldn't say yes, but for the space of a breath, two, three, I feared the answer would not be an unequivocal no.

"You're asking me if I think you would abuse your child?" she said.

Yes. Yes, that was exactly what I was asking her, only I didn't want to put it into words. She was the only one who would *know.* She and my father had known me the longest—until Dan, my mother had known me best. And unlike my husband, who, I was sure, didn't fully see all of my failings or even recognize them as such, my mother never held back her views. I knew she adored me, but when she felt it was warranted, she would tell me the hard truths about who I was. What I lacked. Maybe this was leftover from growing up in her own tumultuous family, but Mom was not only unafraid to call things as she saw them; she didn't know how to do anything else.

"I've always had a temper," I said, and this simple admission, which I wouldn't have so much as blushed at a day before, was now so painful I had to whisper it. "I'm not *patient*."

"We've met, Nicole."

"I get mad, and I yell—what if that's from *her*? What if I'm just angry at my kid all the time? Cindy said our mother was always angry. What if there's—I don't know, a child abuse gene, and she passed it on to me and I hurt my baby?"

"Nicole! You could *never* hurt your child. Or *any* child. You're going to love that little girl more than anything—don't ever doubt that."

My throat ached with tears I wouldn't let fall. I had to keep *some* control, even if my life had become almost unrecognizable. "How do you know?" I whispered.

"Because I have known you your whole life," she said firmly. "Because I'm your mother."

And despite my fear, the guilt I felt for escaping my sister's fate, the lurking evils I now worried were part of my nature, I allowed myself to believe her.

On the last Friday evening in February, Dan and I treated ourselves to takeout from our favorite Chinese restaurant. I broke my fortune cookie in half and read the little slip of paper. *All your hard work is about to pay off.* I slid it across the table to my husband. "Guess I'm about to go into labor!"

I woke up around one in the morning with a bad cramp twisting low in my abdomen. Indigestion, I decided, by now all too familiar with what pregnancy had done to my once reliable stomach, my newly squashed organs. I got myself a second pillow, turned on my left side, and went back to sleep. But as the night progressed, the pain flared and subsided, waking me again and again to stare at the clock on my nightstand. The fifth or sixth time, before I dropped back into a fitful doze, I thought about how strange it was that my indigestion seemed to flare every nine minutes.

By four a.m. I had given up on sleep and the delusion that I might not be in labor. Brenda had promised us that early labor would be "manageable," and so it was. I breathed through what I now knew to be contractions, sitting up in bed with my body still and my heart threatening to run away.

Later, when we told family and friends how this night and day had gone, they would laugh at my choice to let Dan continue sleeping while I labored on my own. I would fire back that I knew I would need him soon enough, and decided one of us, at least, should go into the biggest day of our lives well-rested. But the truth likely had less to do with the kind of clear-eyed pragmatism even labor could not take away from me and more to do with needing time alone, in the darkness and the quiet, to accept that this was happening. There was something special about being the only person who knew our baby was on her way, feeling her scooting ever closer to the world while everybody else slept. In a few hours everyone would know she was almost here, but for now it was still our secret, hers and mine.

When I woke Dan at dawn, ready for some company, he saw that I'd been doing well enough during my silent vigil. The two of us were both fairly calm, united in a sense of purpose: this was the day we had prepared for, trained for. Dan helped me time contractions for a few more hours, writing them all down—what time; how long—on the back of an envelope. We called the birth center when it opened at eight, and I heard Dan chuckling as he spoke with the midwife. Things were moving slowly, I heard him explain; no, her water hasn't broken yet; yes, she says she feels good so far.

Once he had answered all of her questions and hung up, he told me the midwife had predicted a slow and steady labor for us. "She just said, 'First babies,' and laughed," he reported. "They want us to call back when the contractions are about five minutes apart, and come in when you're in active labor. She said be sure to eat; you'll need your strength."

I didn't feel especially hungry, but I munched on some peanut butter toast and then took a shower. Strange, I remember thinking, that a day in labor could begin like any other day. Throughout the morning I moved from position to position, room to room, trying to stay comfortable. Sometimes I walked up and down the stairs; for an hour or two, I straddled a chair and tried to watch a movie. I was tired and not a little terrified, but I also felt encouraged by how easy labor seemed so far. It was a relief to find that our classes, our teacher, and our trusty workbook had not misled us: things would start slow, and build. Naturally.

Hours later, I was a lot less calm. The pain from contractions had moved into my back, and even sitting and rocking on the exercise ball didn't provide much comfort. At our request, our doula had come over to offer support, and the counterpressure she applied to my lower back felt like a gift from God himself. In between contractions—now every six minutes apart—I tried to relax and carry on conversation. Talking made me feel like myself, like I was still in control. I found I often had to grunt, hum, or issue a low groan during the peak of each contraction. Our doula called these "good, productive noises."

The bag for the birth center was already packed in the car, ready to go when we were. The contractions still weren't all that close together, edging closer and closer to five-minute intervals, but the pain was now severe. I hadn't expected so much back labor. Many hours later I would learn it was likely due to our daughter's unusual compound presentation, her arm raised next to her head; in that moment, it felt like more than I could bear for very long. I tried to carry on conversation, but kept slipping into a kind of trance, failing to catch all the words.

So it was with less than total focus that I checked my email around four in the afternoon, sweating and whimpering and desperate for a distraction. My contractions had finally settled at five minutes apart, and Dan was double-checking to make sure we had everything: overnight bag, infant car seat, iPod with my "labor" playlist, snacks and phones and chargers. Refreshing my inbox gave me something to do other than think about the pain. I saw a name in black, bolded Arial, a name that had never before appeared in my list of contacts: CHUNG.

I clicked on the message just as my body seized in another contraction. Words leaped out at me. I knew they must be important, but I couldn't focus on the sentences.

Dear Nicole

I received your letter

please forgive me

My birth father had read my words, looked at my pictures. He had written back immediately—today, of all days. My eyes swam, but it had more to do with pain and fear than emotion. My body wouldn't allow me to focus on anything except the job at hand.

When Dan came back into the house, I closed my laptop and he helped me into my coat. I wanted to tell him about my birth father's email, though I can't remember if I did. I would think of it, off and on, through the long, strange hours that followed. But in this moment, as my husband helped me into the car, news of my birth family didn't seem to belong. It was time for us to meet our baby.

Part III

In the hours following our daughter's birth, the day and night I spent in labor would feel like something someone else had lived through—beginning with the long drive to the birth center in Friday-afternoon rush-hour traffic. At several points I convinced myself it was too hard, too much; I couldn't do this, so somebody else must be doing it for me. I didn't know it at the time, but I was already in transition when we left for the birth center. As the contractions were still five minutes apart, we assumed I must be just on the cusp of active labor.

In the car, though, things felt more intense. Strapped in and unable to bend or move or walk, it was much harder to breathe through the contractions. Dan drove with one hand most of the way, letting me grip his other hand tightly, while the doula followed us in her car. We got stuck behind two school buses. Every bump in the road shuddered through my entire body. Every red light lasted forever. My seat belt seemed too tight, stretched across a body that now felt possessed, but I was afraid to unfasten it.

We finally made it to the birth center around five o'clock, daylight giving way to winter dusk. Jenny, the midwife on call, brought us to the Blue Room, a homey birthing room with pale blue walls and ocean-themed pictures. She checked me quickly and said, "You're eight centimeters dilated and one hundred percent effaced!" I couldn't believe it. At home, we had thought I was only four or five centimeters dilated "at most," based on the timing and how I had seemed during contractions. "What a great job you're doing! See how prepared you were?"

I allowed myself to feel optimistic; transition was supposed to be the hardest stage of labor, and I did feel I was managing it well so far. But nine months of pregnancy and all our books and classes had not taken away my fear of birth itself. Of crowning, and pushing, and giving way to new, insistent life.

I was able to talk in between contractions, so that's what I did—partly as a distraction; partly because it was reassuring to still feel like myself. I remember babbling at the nurse and midwife about my labor playlist. Our doula stood behind me, continuing—thank god—to apply pressure to my spasming lower back, while Dan supported my weight, counting me down from the contractions. "You're doing so well," he told me, over and over; "you're getting so close." I held on to his words. As hard as it was to bear, the pain *did* have a purpose. It would end soon.

But the pain escalated while dilation slowed, then halted. Hours passed, a second nurse came on call, and still I was only at eight and a half centimeters. I'd endured many long, agonizing hours of transition, which was supposed to be the shortest stage of labor. We all knew that if labor had proceeded as expected, I would already have given birth. The intense back labor seemed to concern Jenny, who wondered if the baby might be in a bad position for delivery.

We had met all the midwives in the practice over months of prenatal appointments, and while they all seemed wonderful, Jenny was one of my favorites. She was quiet and unruffled and professional; something in her kind, elfin face also reminded me of a dear college friend. So when she sat on the edge of the bed and asked whether I might be scared (of course I was) and if there was anything the birth team could do to help me push through this last phase, I gripped her hand and didn't cry, even though I wanted to. I wasn't scared for our baby—we kept checking for signs of distress, and she was holding up like a champ. But I was so discouraged, and I didn't know how much more I could endure.

When I finally made it to ten centimeters and got the go-ahead to push, it felt like such a relief, a miracle in itself, I wanted to laugh. Time slowed to the point of having little meaning. I made myself focus on just getting through one more contraction, and then one more minute; when even a minute seemed like too much, I lived second to second. Though I couldn't quite focus on his face or register his words, I knew Dan was telling me how much he loved me and our baby; how proud he was of us. How he knew that it was hard, but I could do it. If he was scared, or worn-out, plagued with doubt, no one would have known.

If it were up to me, I knew I would have long since given up. I'd been in labor for nearly twenty-four hours; I was exhausted, digging deep for every push, and had no energy of my own left. But I felt as if someone else's will to be born had taken over.

"You're doing *great*, Nicole," Jenny said suddenly, and these seemed like the first clear words I had heard in hours. "One, maybe two more pushes and she'll be born!"

It was the most powerful moment of my life, that moment shortly after one in the morning when I heard her cry and knew she was finally with us. Our daughter decided to come into the world with one fist raised. Seconds later she was placed on my chest, beautiful and flushed and still screaming at the shock of birth, and I touched her hair, her warm little cheek. Her skin felt impossibly soft, softer than I knew anything could be.

At seven pounds, fifteen ounces, twenty inches long, she was not a small baby—her wails were also lusty, much louder than I'd expected—but she felt new and fragile in my arms. She stopped crying and gazed up at me, and my world shrank to the arresting dark blue pools of her eyes. It was such a strange color, I thought—I had never seen anyone with eyes like that. In a few days, I suspected, they would darken to brown, but for now I reveled in their uniqueness. Her skin, ruddy from birth, would likewise settle into a shade that nearly matched mine. She was born with a tiny bump of a nose—I recognized it as my own in almost comic miniature. My chin. The shape of my eyes. A look on her face that I recognized, one that struck me as already *impatient* to know and explore and understand.

As I looked at her, I knew the person I had been was gone, unmade in an instant by this tiny girl. The rebuilding, I was certain, would take a lifetime.

"Do you have a name picked out?" Jenny asked us.

Dan and I had spent hours talking about names, digging through books and searching our own memories for favorites. For a few weeks I even toyed with the idea of suggesting the name Susan, after I learned it was the name my birth parents had picked out for me, but then dismissed the idea—it felt like too much to lay on a newborn's tiny shoulders. I did not want her to imagine that I had her only because I'd been given up; that I expected her to live out her life with us the way I might have with my original family. She wasn't here to make me feel complete or make up for the choices of others. She was here because we loved her.

Dan and I had chosen a favorite name years before we had even thought about starting a family. After all this time, it was still the one we both wanted for her. Abigail nursed, then fell asleep on my chest, content in the swaddle the nurse had expertly wrapped her in. Dan slept, too, after calling our families. I had never been so tired, and I was sore to the very roots of my hair, but I couldn't seem to close my eyes—how could anyone expect me to sleep when I had this fascinating little face to watch? It was almost impossible to believe this was the same unseen being who'd done jumping jacks on my bladder, greeting me with kicks and pokes and slow stretches for weeks on end. She was so small and so *new*, barely and yet wholly herself, already.

As I looked at our daughter, sleeping peacefully in her swaddle and her flannel hat, I felt a little bad that she'd been forced into clothing after months of being tucked up safe and warm. Moments after my own birth, I'd been moved from someone's arms to the impersonal if life-sustaining embrace of the incubator. I wondered if my mother had gotten a chance to hold me. Had she even wanted to? Had she seen me after the crisis, the premature birth, before the adoption? Had my father ever seen me again?

My daughter would always know me. She would never have to fight to know her story. She would never have to wonder if we had loved her, wanted her. Suddenly I remembered the words of a friend and fellow adopted daughter, also a parent of young children: *I love telling my kids their birth stories. It's such a privilege to be able to do that.*

Yes, I thought, *and also a miracle.* The clichéd word didn't embarrass me; this day and night was a wonder I'd never get over. As many times as this had happened before, to billions of parents since time immemorial, it was the only time it had ever happened to me. I had a child now, and she was mine. We were together. We would *stay* together.

When Abby was old enough to ask me—to wonder, and to listen, and to care—I would tell her about her birth, her first days with us. *You were born with one arm raised, which wasn't very nice*, I would say. *When it was over, you and Daddy slept, but I couldn't. All I wanted to do was look at you.*

Cindy, thank you so much for the teddy bear you sent! Please thank Rick for us, too. I'm sure Abby will love it when she is interested in something besides milk.

I've never felt so inadequate, so exhausted, or so glad. We're still trying to establish some semblance of a daily pattern, and when she cries I can't help but feel I am failing her somehow. I knew it would be hard. But I am aware this season is brief and soon she'll be different—less needy—and I'll be glad and also wistful to see her grow. She's changing so fast; already she is so much bigger and more herself than she was when we first brought her home. She has my chubby cheeks and a dimple in her ear that came from her daddy. She has hair that sticks out a little, just like mine. She likes to rest against my chest, use her strong little arms to push herself up, and crane her neck to stare up at me for a few seconds before she loses control of her head. She watches me as if she expects me to reveal the secrets of the universe. She watches as if she could understand me if I did.

Everyone told me she looked like Dan. While I thought so, too, at times it still stung. I'd waited so long to see our shared inheritance spelled out in the shape of her eyes, the curl of her hands, her fast-dawning facial expressions.

I could see Dan's influence, of course, without even trying. But I saw myself, too, every time I looked at her. She and I had the same full cheeks, though hers were chubbier than mine. Her keen eyes did turn a deep, dark brown, and when she closed them in sleep she reminded me of photos I'd seen—me, as a baby, sleeping on my new parents' chests. It was incredible to see so many well-known features blended in one small face; to watch a smile I thought of as more my husband's chased across her face by a look of confusion or consternation that was all me. It all made me wonder how much I had looked like my birth parents as a baby. I wondered if I would ever have the chance to ask either of them.

New parenthood was a blur of sleeplessness and soreness and wonder, of dramatic milestones and timed feedings mostly contained within the four robin's-egg-blue walls of our bedroom. Abigail's bassinet was hooked to the side of our bed, where she slept, sometimes swaddled, in between feedings and diaper changes. We became adept at changing her on a changing pad on the bed and quickly transferring her to my arms for a feeding in the rocking chair. She liked to fall asleep on my chest, or on Dan's, but once awake would dig her little arm in and push her head back so she could stare into our faces. I got the distinct impression she wanted to communicate with us already. I had no frame of reference for any of the shocking physical sensations of motherhood—the jolt I felt close to my heart when she cried, needing food only I could provide; the satisfaction that unfurled through me when she fell asleep in my arms; the bone-deep tiredness of sleep deprivation and giving over my body and my mind to this entirely new endeavor. Everything was somehow unexpected, even when I should have expected it.

My parents had met me when I was two and a half months old. They didn't spend nine months anticipating or preparing for my birth; they didn't experience the high drama of labor or those sweet moments of relief just after delivery. As Dan and I learned how to take care of our newborn, I wondered if my parents had ever felt cheated out of so many of my firsts—by the time they brought me home, someone else had changed my first diaper, caught my first funny stares and smiles, taught me to drink from a bottle. I couldn't imagine missing a moment of Abby's early life. How long it had taken for them to feel like my real parents?

After a week or so, she was already a different baby than the one we'd brought home, so sleepy and fussy because we didn't know how to swaddle and bounce her *the right way*. In time she noticed her own reflection in the crib mirror, and began babbling at it. She couldn't control her hands at all, but whenever they landed on something, the textures fascinated her endlessly. She began to wake us up not just with cries in the middle of the night, but coos and gurgles in the morning—sounds that were strangely conversational, reminding me of my dad's old line. *She's talking to her angels*, I thought.

One morning a week after the birth, I righted her after a feeding in bed and had barely started to pat her back when she spat up all over herself and the bedspread. Dan, who was also awake, leaped up to find some burp cloths and towels. I shook my head at Abigail, who was now screaming. "Thanks for missing my ponytail," I told her.

Suddenly my phone rang. I didn't recognize the number. Deciding this was my exit from the current situation, I shifted our daughter into Dan's arms and accepted the call, ignoring my husband's incredulous look. *Seriously?* his eyes seemed to be asking. *Now?*

"Nicole?" She spoke the two syllables of my name as if they were her first, hesitant sounds in a foreign language. "This is your mother."

For an instant, I was too tired and shocked to feel anything. When an emotion did sweep in, it was irritation—and guilt, because I did not want to talk to her. Hadn't I asked Jessica to tell her I just gave birth, and wasn't ready to talk? Jessica probably had, I guessed, and she had just decided to call me anyway.

But whatever she had done, she was my mother, and I had been the one to go looking for her. Still holding a partially digested milk–encrusted burp cloth in my hand, struggling to hear over the sound of my baby crying, for a few seconds I tried not to think about everything I'd learned. I tried not to feel annoyed that she'd called a week after I had given birth, after I had specifically said that *I* wanted to call *her* when I was ready. I opened my mouth to thank her for calling, marshaling the kind of manners that would have earned an approving nod from my grandmother. *I'm so sorry,* I could say, *now just isn't a good time.*

But she offered me an apology first, cutting off my own. "I'm sorry," she said, "so sorry to you."

Oh, Jesus, I thought. *What to say to* that? And then a realization: *She sounds nothing like me.*

It was true. I'd never sound like her, even decades from now. Her voice sounded oddly heavy; thick, but not with emotion. Cool and calm and direct. Just the few words she had spoken were enough to reveal traces of a heavy accent.

My mind spun. She was apologizing to *me?* Did she have me confused with Cindy, the daughter she'd kept and the one she'd raised, the one to whom she'd given bruises where they wouldn't show and a fear she had never outgrown? Cindy wasn't sure she ever wanted children, and our mother was the reason. *I don't know if I can ever have kids,* she told me after Abby was born, *but I'm thrilled to be an aunt to yours.*

Across the room, Dan could not have missed my expression, the sudden—what? Panic?—in my eyes. *Who is it?* he mouthed while bouncing on the balls of his feet, falling into the gentle dance we'd learned almost before anything else, the one we both did unconsciously when trying to get Abby to settle down. I shook my head— it was too hard to explain with the phone glued to my ear—tossed the burp cloth into the laundry basket, and went downstairs.

I wanted to interrupt my mother's string of apologies, but what would I say if I did? I paced from living room to kitchen to dining room and around again, circling the first floor of our house and listening to my mother's voice—waiting for questions about me, about my life, that never came. I didn't have to know her in order to register the shame in her voice. It was a voice as unlike mine as any stranger's, older and harder and still, after thirty years in America, uneasy with the only language I had ever comfortably spoken.

"I wanted to keep you," she said. "I'm so sorry."

"Please don't worry about it," I tried to say, when she paused to take a breath. My words felt generous, given what I knew of her, and also deeply inadequate. "You did what you thought was best for me."

"No," she said. "I never wanted to give you away. It was all his idea, your father. He forced me to sign. I didn't want to."

My heart lurched. Whether this was true or not, I knew what kind of parent she had been. She wasn't the person I had been told about, the one I had always imagined. I wanted to say something in anger, have it out with her like I might have with my own mom.

But *I never wanted to give you away* were the words I'd always wanted to hear from her, from my birth father. It was the closest I'd ever come to being told one of them wanted me. She couldn't know how many times I'd tried to imagine hearing these words from her as a child, as a woman, an expectant mother. Couldn't know how badly I'd hoped to hear that some part of her regretted giving me away.

I had always intended to tell her she made the right decision. That it was all right; that I understood why she had done it. Yet that pleasant fiction, that lie about parents who had loved me so much they had to give me away, had never been precisely true. This woman had never felt about me the way I felt about my daughter. To her, I was fairly certain, I had been a complication in an existing tangle of misery; a problem that had to be solved.

She kept saying that my birth father had forced her hand, and I wondered how he'd managed to impose his will over my fate given that he couldn't stop her from hitting my sister. What sort of power had they exerted over each other, these two people stuck in their wretched marriage? He stayed with her for years, though she was beating their youngest child. She agreed to the adoption, though she claimed she had never wanted to. This much I could almost believe—in her account, in his letter to me, in the social worker's notes, the adoption was always his idea. But why didn't she just agree readily? Why not be grateful he had suggested the adoption; why not sign at once, without protest?

Maybe she was telling the truth now. Maybe she *had* wanted me. And what if she hadn't wanted to place me for adoption, and he had? People were not so simple; people could be and think and want many different things at once. What if terrorizing my sister had seemed, in some twisted way, natural or understandable to her—*I'm your mother, you just have to take what I give you*—whereas giving me away, losing that same measure of absolute control over me, had not? She might have had not one, but two little girls in her home. I might have grown up feeling just as afraid of her as my sister had. Perhaps some part of her hadn't wanted me, but hadn't wanted someone *else* to have me, either.

No one could be a bad parent in all the ways it was possible to be bad. It was one thing to hit a child, and another to be willing to give one away like an old sofa or a coat you had outgrown. The first, to me, seemed far worse than the second. But in a sense, it didn't really matter what she had wanted at the time. If she *had* wanted to keep me, for whatever reason—if she hesitated to sign the adoption papers and felt my absence more deeply than did my birth father—that didn't necessarily make her the better, more devoted parent.

Anger, hot and fierce and tinged with something new, some heretofore foreign maternal instinct, spiked in my chest. I wanted to lash out, remind her of how she'd treated the daughter she hadn't given up. *That's* what you should be sorry for, I wanted to tell her, fighting past her momentarily disarming words. *That's* what you should regret. I thought about breaking into her litany of apologies, the accusations directed at her ex-husband, and telling her everything I knew. *I know she used to hide, lock herself in the bathroom, run away from home just to get away from you. I know you told her my "death" was her fault, because she upset you on the day I was born. I know the truth, and so does Cindy. Have you ever apologized to* her?

My birth mother asked, her voice a little plaintive, if I had ever thought about moving back to the west coast. Or, if I did not move back, could I visit sometime?

Again, I did not know what to say. I could no longer imagine meeting her, and I didn't want to tell her that. For some reason, I kept thinking of what Jessica had told me in one of her emails: *Mom has had a really hard life.* She eventually shared that our mother's own father had been abusive, especially when he'd been drinking. Out of seven siblings, she was the only one who seemed to have inherited, by example or by genetics, her father's hot temper and harsh ways. Both Jessica and Cindy told me that when she was not upset, she was a different person; she could be funny and charming. But when she was angry, she never had control.

What was the point of railing against my birth mother after all these years? Would she even understand the source of my anger on behalf of my sister, or would it just be one more thing she blamed on Cindy? I was years too late to help anyone. I was not even part of this family. My fury and anguish meant nothing.

"I really have to go," I said. Upstairs, my daughter was crying, and while I knew she was fine with Dan, I wanted to be with her; to press my nose into her soft, wispy baby curls and tell her I loved her again. It would be many months before she would be able to understand the words, but I hoped she already knew. "I promise, I don't blame you for the adoption. I don't think it was your fault."

It was true. I didn't blame her. I finally understood what my birth parents did not: my adoption was hard, and complicated, but it was not a tragedy. It was not my fault, and it wasn't theirs, either. It was the easiest way to solve just one of too many problems.

And apart from this, I could not offer my birth mother a single thing—I could not commit to a relationship, or the visit she had asked me for. I couldn't give her peace. I couldn't even offer her forgiveness, because it wasn't mine to give. Her real wrongdoings, acknowledged or not, had so little to do with me.

"If you cannot visit soon, will you call sometime?" she asked.

I tried to imagine it. Picking up the phone and dialing, hoping to hear her voice, longing for it instead of dreading it. If I had ever been hers—and if she had been the parent I imagined her to be—her voice could have been one of comfort, the voice I grew up hearing in my darkest or most joyful moments. I would have called her when I discovered I was pregnant. I would have called minutes after Abby was born. I had a loving family, and they had been there for these and so many other milestones in my life, moments of sadness and moments of triumph. For all her flaws and all of mine, I wondered if any part of my birth mother still grieved for all the things she had missed, things it was too late for us to share.

"I don't know when I'll call." It was the only answer I could give her. It was also the truth. There was nothing else to say, I realized—not even a question of hers I could answer, because she hadn't asked me anything about myself. "Thank you for calling. Goodbye."

She was quiet. I had to check my phone to make sure the call had ended. I dropped the phone on the couch and went to find my husband and daughter. As I told Dan about the strange conversation, it occurred to me that my birth mother had never said goodbye. In the end, she'd simply disappeared.

All my life, I'd had no biological relatives at all—none that I knew, anyway—and now I had a baby, another set of parents I couldn't understand, and a sister who wrote to me daily. My birth father had written to me, too: the email he sent the day I went into labor. Weeks went by in a postpartum haze, day bleeding into night and back into day, and still I had not responded to him.

In his letter, my birth father told me he knew, even before I was born so early, that my birth mother wouldn't take good care of me. He also said that the adoption was his suggestion.

She said she didn't want another baby, so I said, why not give the baby to someone who wants her?

I noticed he never said that *he* wanted me.

I wanted to write back to him, but for what felt like one long, continuous day, all Dan and I could do was meet Abigail's needs and take care of ourselves. *This is nighttime,* I remember telling our daughter, standing at the living room window and showing her how dark and quiet it was outside. *This is when we sleep.* Overwhelmed by caring for a newborn, I asked Cindy to let our father know that I would write back as soon as I could set aside the time for a proper response. He didn't have my phone number yet, and I don't think I offered it, still recovering from my birth mother's call.

That we'd made contact just as my own baby arrived put my birth parents at a kind of disadvantage. I knew that I would do anything for my child; that no situation, however desperate or dire, would make me willing to give up the privilege of being her mother. All of this was less because she was *mine*, and more because she was her own, already: now that we had met, I could not imagine *not* knowing her.

In the emotional throes of new motherhood, the hours I spent caring for my baby, puzzling out whatever I felt for my birth parents, whatever they meant to me, seemed such a daunting task. My birth parents could not have been to me what I was to Abigail, I thought. They had left me and they hadn't even known I would be okay. They had denied the very fact of my life. As a parent, I was incapable of such a thing, and I knew it—now that my daughter was here, I knew my life wouldn't make any sense without her. Not a day, maybe not even a waking hour, would pass empty of some thought of her.

In his letter, my birth father told me about his work, his interests, his volunteer work with his church, how he helped more recent immigrants settle here in their new country. He said he was proud of me (*for what?* I wondered, more curious than skeptical; so far all he knew was that I'd gone to college, gotten married, and had a baby). Like my birth mother, he apologized and begged my forgiveness. He said he had also asked God for forgiveness. Of all the things to regret, I thought, why the choice that had likely saved me? I could not think of my adoption as a sin, and wanted to tell him that it wasn't necessary; to remind him that Cindy had gone through far worse—but it felt wrong, somehow, to think of inserting myself into the maelstrom of his emotions, whatever they were, or push my way into a family drama that began before and continued long after I disappeared from their lives.

149

My birth parents' memories seemed to be based on what each wished to believe, and I couldn't quite reconcile their stories. The two of them seemed united in one belief only: what happened all those years ago when I was born was beyond their control; it had simply happened *to* them, an event ruled by unfeeling fate. Beyond that, they were each convinced the other had no care whatsoever for my well-being, and had simply acted selfishly. They could not both be right; either one of them didn't know the truth, or one of them was lying. Was I to believe the woman who hurt her daughter, or the man who said I was dead? The woman who'd tried to reach out to me when I was a child, or the man who told me he wept when he saw my picture?

If they felt so ashamed for giving me up, after all this time—even after I told them there was no need—did that mean *I* should be ashamed of it as well? I could not see my way to it. I had never been taught to hold on to guilt or shame, especially after a thing had been acknowledged, confessed. From the time I was young, I had assumed the same truth that freed me would also free my birth family—that the rush of air and light sweeping away the secrets would come as a relief to all of us. If I learned one thing in the early days of our reunion, it was that I could not compel another person to feel comforted, to feel whole, to forgive themselves. The peace I'd wanted so badly to give my birth parents, all along, was never in my power to give.

In one of her letters, Cindy said she felt she understood me because she got the feeling I was "searching for the truth, too." She was right, though in more honest moments I could admit that I'd have preferred a truth closer to the shiny, sanitized fantasy I'd entertained as a child—the dignified, self-sacrificing immigrant ideal that had been cooked up for me by others. More than once I had even imagined sitting down with my birth parents for a civilized meal and a long, cleansing chat—our interactions would remain mature, light, and friendly; on my side, almost journalistic. At the end of our conversation, I would say goodbye and leave them, finally understanding all I'd ever hoped to understand.

Of our two parents, I was now far more inclined to trust my birth father—because of my new relationship with Cindy. But that didn't mean I felt ready to leap into a relationship with him, assuming he would even want one. I didn't feel comfortable asking for many explanations now. I wasn't sure how much I wanted to let him into my life. It was different for Cindy. They were family, and had lived through what my birth father called "those dark days" together. If she wanted the truth, she was his real daughter; perhaps she had a right to demand it.

The only right I felt *I* had, now, was to accept what I could not know and retreat. And while I'd been caught up in the Korean soap opera that had become my life, I knew it was also in my power to end it. To step back from my birth family, and let time and distance pull us apart once more. *And maybe*, I thought, *that's exactly what I ought to do.*

*Watching your baby learn how to do something new, you no-
tice all the little movements that go into, say, a roll—from the
instant she decides she might just make the effort, to the slow
testing of the space around her, to the planting of one leg, the
swinging of another, the final bit of strength that allows her to
push against the floor and pick her head back up. Yesterday—for
the first time—she rolled from her back to her tummy, pushing
off from the ground with one foot, swinging her leg up and over,
planting it on the floor to stabilize herself, pulling her arms out
from under her, lifting her head and chest back up, catching my
eye long enough to grin at me with false modesty:* What are you
staring at? I do this all the time.

*She is getting more and more expressive, always trying out new
faces—variations on what I call Abigail's Look of the Day. I am
constantly amazed by how many of these looks seem cribbed
from my face. Yesterday she took my face between her hands and
said, very seriously, "Mom," and then broke into a huge grin.
She is so pleased with herself when she makes wordlike sounds,
though I know she has no idea what she's saying. But she smiles
her biggest and widest for me, and I go to enormous lengths to
hear her bright staccato laugh.*

Even if it was hard to know what to think or
do about my birth parents, it was easy and
wonderful to write to Cindy. As I updated her
on the life and times of her niece at a few months old, I found myself wondering what she had been like as a little girl. Did she look
like me (or, as the youngest, had *I* looked like *her*)? Would we have
played well together, liked each other as children? We joked that we

152

couldn't possibly keep writing at this rate, but it became clear that neither of us wanted to slow down. We had nearly three decades' worth of stories and confidences to cram into our correspondence, after all; it felt like there was no time to waste.

When you are growing up adopted, people like to tell you how lucky you are. Having learned the truth about my birth family, I couldn't disagree. But it wasn't so simple: there are many different kinds of luck; many different ways to be blessed or cursed. And if I had been lucky in the parents who raised me, maybe now I could be lucky again—I felt so happy that, for the rest of my life, these early days of motherhood would be inextricably linked with my first memories of Cindy.

I don't know how you would have been treated if you'd stayed with us, Nikki, but I know your sisters would have loved you and tried to protect you. We would have shared things we could not share with our parents. We would have shared funny stories in those awful times. We would have promised each other that no one would get between us.

I often read her emails, sent from three hours behind, in the middle of the night while Abby nursed. If I wrote back to her in those hours, I knew I'd probably receive an answer before noon my time, sent before she left for work in the morning. While our letters couldn't close the gap of geography and lost memory, the miles and the years between us, in snippets and snapshots I was getting to know her. She described herself as "shy," but in writing, she wasn't—and there was something in her directness and her curiosity that I found comforting and oddly familiar.

Early on, we both hinted at the possibility of a visit, but then never formed a solid plan—in part because I gave birth, in part because Cindy had to schedule her vacation from the medical clinic months in advance. When Abby was four or five months old, I realized I had yet to actually invite my sister and her husband to our house. I'd said things like *We'd love to meet you* and *You're always more than welcome to visit* to both her and Jessica, and they weren't just polite words; I meant them. But I had never offered specific dates or told Cindy when would be a good time for us. I had never asked her to look at her calendar and let me know what would work for her and Rick. I had never *asked* them to come, and she hadn't asked if they could.

In the back of my mind, I'd begun to worry that perhaps she hadn't asked because she didn't want to meet me after all. My fear was not that Cindy would actively dislike me, but that she would decide she could do just as well without me—as, indeed, she had for most of her life. She hadn't grown up, as I had, wishing or imagining that she had a sister. Her childhood had been about endurance, finding the strength to get through another day; and that, she'd explained, had made her into a survivor: someone who could, like and also unlike her parents, compartmentalize and leave people behind when needed. *We can cut people off*, she had once written, *and not look back. We do what we have to do.*

I wasn't going to be content with emails and calls forever. But what if that was really all she wanted? Or what if we met in person and I disappointed her? She didn't owe me anything; bonds that might have held us together over a lifetime had been broken, and we could rebuild them only through choice and mutual effort. Eventually the initial thrill of discovering her long-lost sister would fade, and then she would have to decide on a relationship with me based on me alone. I was sure I was not as good as she was, as strong as she was.

When I confessed my worry to Dan, though, he pointed at the dozens of emails in my growing "Cindy" folder. "She wouldn't be writing to you every single day if she didn't want to know you."

Maybe, I thought then, my sister was waiting for *me*. Waiting for a sign, or at least an invitation. I thought of something Rick had written in an email, days after Cindy first contacted me. *I have always felt that Cindy has never been given the love that she deserves.*

She was never given anything. Just like me, Cindy might be managing her expectations; Rick had said she was used to being let down. But I didn't want her to fear that I would let her down, too.

We should plan that visit, I ventured one day. *Do you want to fly out and stay with us?*

Her reply landed in my inbox in a matter of hours. *When can we come?*

A month before her planned visit, and two days after my daughter's first birthday, Cindy called to tell me she was pregnant. I don't remember what I said after "Congratulations!" but I remember that my happiness—and her eagerness to share the news with me, the very day she learned she was pregnant—felt like a harbinger of the kind of relationship I hoped we'd have. "I'm going to be an *aunt*!" I told Dan, and then everyone else I knew.

Early in our correspondence, Cindy had told me she wasn't sure she ever wanted children. *I get pressure from my dad and stepmom to have a child, and sometimes it drives me crazy.* She never genuinely believed she would end up like her mother, but it was hard to imagine having her own family after everything she had been through. Recalling my late-night call to my mother, the reassurance I'd pulled from her regarding my own capacity to love and care for my child, I could understand why Cindy was anxious.

In the months that followed our new connection, however— months during which the bulk of my correspondence included some news about Abby, and who she was becoming in her first year of life—Cindy admitted to feeling less certain. She had gone off the

Pill. *Every day*, she said, *I tell myself I am not our mom. I tell myself I will not make the same mistakes. Maybe I'll give myself a chance if we do become pregnant.* I couldn't imagine her being anything but a wonderful parent, and—thinking of what my mother's words had meant to me—I told her so.

Three days after she told me she was pregnant, Cindy went to the doctor and found out that her HCG levels were dropping. Probably a miscarriage, she was told.

But an ultrasound revealed something more alarming: an ectopic pregnancy. The doctor gave her a choice: she could take injections of methotrexate to end the pregnancy, or undergo laparoscopic surgery to remove the embryo from her fallopian tube. Cindy decided to try the former. After their loss, she told me, she and Rick knew they really did want to have a child, and the injections were the least invasive option.

I asked how she was, feeling helpless. *Sad*, she wrote, *but I will be okay.* I wished I could be there to help, or just be with her. It had been a wretched few days, Cindy said, but she and Rick had plenty of support. They were grieving, and they would get through this together.

She needed to have frequent lab draws to test her HCG levels and make sure they continued to fall, including one just before their trip out to see us. I promised I would understand if she and Rick decided to postpone their trip. *I'll be okay to travel*, she insisted. We were two weeks out from her visit. *I've been looking forward to this for too long.*

The day before they were to leave, Rick called me early in the morning. It was five a.m. in Portland, I realized. I answered with dread that I tried to keep out of my voice.

The previous afternoon, Cindy had gone back to her ob-gyn and learned that the injections of methotrexate had failed to resolve the ectopic pregnancy. Her doctor insisted she couldn't travel as she was; she needed to be closely monitored until they were certain the pregnancy had ended and she was in no danger. Cindy asked if she could go on the trip if she had the surgery instead.

Theoretically, she was told with raised eyebrows, though it would be better to postpone and give the injections a chance to work. They'd been treating Cindy for weeks; this was the first they'd heard about travel plans. Yes, the pregnancy needed to end, but this seemed rash. "Can't you just postpone your vacation?" the nurse asked.

Cindy felt angry now, but she didn't want to argue with the nurse. She directed her plea to the doctor, who had always struck her as capable and kind. "Listen," she said, "this isn't just any vacation. This is really important."

The doctor asked for the room. When they were alone, she said, "Tell me more."

So Cindy told her about the sister who had been adopted, the one she had long believed dead. They had been planning this visit for months. Cindy might not be able to take another full week off until the following year. "I just feel like this might be my one shot," she said. "I *have* to go."

That meant she had to have surgery tonight.

The ob-gyn couldn't pretend she was pleased by the prospect of her patient leaving on a cross-country trip immediately after surgery, but she agreed to scrub up. It was midnight by the time the ectopic pregnancy was removed, via the laparoscopic surgery Cindy had so hoped to avoid. Afterward, the nurse tried again: "You know you shouldn't go on this trip. We can't monitor you from across the country."

But the doctor could see that Cindy was committed to going, even if they could not guarantee her safety. Rick was to bring Cindy's painkillers, watch her closely, take her to urgent care if necessary. They were to call and get help immediately if any one of half a dozen symptoms occurred.

"Of course we want to see you both, but Cindy just had surgery!" I said after Rick told me what had happened. "You know we'd understand if you wanted to wait."

"She says we can't. It'd be too hard for her to get more time off." This was only the second or third time we'd ever spoken, but he sounded so weary.

"What did the doctor say?"

Rick laughed a little. "Oh, the doctor's not happy." He still sounded worried, but another note had crept into his voice—one of resignation, determined calm. He wanted to reassure *me*, I realized. He had already accepted his wife's decision. "Cin made it really clear that she's going. I will be her walking pharmacy."

As much as I wanted to see them, see *her*, I tried one more time. "You don't have to do this. Cindy shouldn't put her health at risk. Maybe we can come and see you instead, once she's—"

"Nikki. Do you have any idea how stubborn your sister is? Oh, I guess you don't." My brother-in-law laughed again, this time sounding more like the jovial man I'd spoken with before—the one who had emailed me days into my long-distance acquaintance with Cindy, to relay history and friendly jokes and what I only later recognized as a thinly veiled warning. He had wanted me to understand how special Cindy was—and that she was no longer alone, in case it turned out I wanted something she shouldn't have to give. He wanted me to know that he was looking out for her.

"I'll make sure she gets to you in one piece," Rick promised. "We will see you soon."

The discussion, I understood, was over. Not because of Rick, or because of me, but because the iron will of my still-sleeping sister had imposed itself. None of us were looking back now. *See, that's one thing you have in common already*, Dan would say later, when I told him the visit was still on. *She's as stubborn as you are.*

Confined to our porch by a steady spring shower, I gazed out from under the eaves and watched a car go by. Another car that wasn't theirs. I considered going back inside, waiting patiently with my husband and daughter, but allowing Cindy to walk up to the door and ring our bell like a stranger would require an unthinkable level of calm.

Rick had texted me briefly, letting me know they had arrived, but he hadn't mentioned how the flights had gone or how Cindy was faring after the long day of travel. Given that she had been in the operating room only the day before yesterday, I couldn't help but worry that the trip had been too much for her, too soon. Still, worry couldn't compete with my nerves or excitement—any moment now, their rental car would be pulling up to our house, and I would finally see my sister.

A car appeared around the bend in the road, driving slowly, headlights on, windshield wipers swishing. When it turned into our driveway, I bounded from the porch and ran out to meet them without a raincoat or umbrella. I caught my first glimpse of Cindy's face through the passenger window, her features blurred on the other side of the rain-streaked glass, and for an instant I could almost imagine that I was gazing at my own reflection in a strange, enchanted mirror.

Then her door swung open and our arms were around each other.

Remembering her stitches, I tried not to grip too tightly—but I couldn't seem to let go of her. Fat raindrops dotted my red sweater, mingled with the moisture on my face. I didn't care that I was getting wet. All I could think was that I was just weeks away from turning twenty-eight, and I was hugging my big sister for the first time.

I don't know how long we held on before I pulled back to look at her, trying to read pain or exhaustion in her face. The trip must have been awful for her, but she wasn't complaining; she seemed glad to be here. I saw no regret on her face, but there was, perhaps, just a hint of the same trepidation I felt. Like me, Cindy was dressed in long sleeves and jeans, her zip-up jacket a deep purple that I knew by now was one of her favorite colors. She kept it on when we went into the house, though even with the rain it was a warm spring day; eventually she would admit to me that she was always cold.

Our eyes, I saw up close, looked to be about the same hue. Her hair was perhaps a shade closer to true black than mine, fewer dark browns mixed in, but from a distance it would appear the same color. When she smiled, especially, she was more beautiful than I had ever believed myself to be.

Rick and I hugged, too, and once inside we had another round of hugs with Dan and Abby. My daughter, usually so shy among strangers, basked in the attention. Dan was quietly happy for us, grinning in his usual way; Rick appeared to be almost quivering with excitement, holding back to give Cindy and me a chance to fill the initial silence ourselves.

But someone else couldn't pick up on the cues in the room, and didn't realize what this moment meant. As soon as Cindy sat down on the light blue sofa, Abby began bringing her toys to admire and well-chewed board books to read aloud. Usually it took our daughter several hours if not days to warm up to new people, to refrain from fussing if they tried to pick her up. Yet she hesitated only seconds before plopping down next to Cindy, smiling shyly while her aunt read to her. I could tell my sister was charmed.

"She likes you, Cin," Rick told her. "Maybe it's because you look exactly like her mom."

Not exactly. I could not help but correct him, though I only did so silently. Still, it was true that Abby had never seen anyone who resembled me as much as Cindy. As I watched her read, I suddenly found myself thinking, somewhat nonsensically, *My sister has freckles.*

They were a surprise. Why were they a surprise? I suppose I hadn't spotted the pale brown freckles in any of the photos. All I'd ever had were scattered birthmarks: tiny chocolate-brown dots on my cheeks, a larger one on my chin, a few more up and down my arms. My sister had those, too, plenty of them, but she also had a dusting of real freckles on her face. *They're adorable*, I thought.

I wondered if Abby might end up having freckles, too.

The differences didn't end there. From pictures, I already knew that Cindy's face was slightly rounder than mine, her cheekbones more prominent, her nose a tad narrower, her eyes not so wide-set. Many of her features were just close enough to mine to clearly point to our connection, but not so close that we would ever be mistaken for each other. She was thinner, and I was taller, though we'd already ascertained that we wore the same size. Cindy's less-hurried movements made me feel rushed and overlarge and awkward next to her.

It was the difference in our voices that struck me most. We had spoken on the phone before, so perhaps I should have been prepared for it, but in person—maybe because she was tired, or because she was still recovering from her surgery—Cindy was even more soft-spoken; I imagined I'd had *thoughts* louder than some of her words. She didn't strike me as meek or passive, just quiet—and, like Dan, more accustomed to watching and listening than speaking without thought, as I did far too often. When she did interject a word here or there, her voice was far less direct or excitable than her husband's or mine.

I must seem so loud and brash to her, I thought, falling silent.

Was I *too much* for her? I doubted that Cindy was expecting to find a calm or demure person after the year we'd spent corresponding. Still, I wondered if I would annoy her; if she would even *like* me by the time the week was out.

For my part, I liked her natural reserve—it was part of who she was. But that made it difficult to tell how she was feeling, whereas I felt sure my emotions had to be obvious, raw as they were and close to surface. Should I say something about it, openly acknowledge the tension in the room instead of reaching for small talk? Or would that just overwhelm her?

Much as I had looked forward to meeting my sister, I still didn't know what to expect now that she had arrived. I couldn't pretend there was anything typical about this. When I decided to try to reunite with my birth family, I was given no guide for what to do or say the first time we saw each other. What if, for all our shared genes, we had nothing in common? What if my adoption and all the years of separation proved too great a distance for curiosity and good intentions to bridge?

I'm so sorry they never told you about me. It must have come as the biggest shock.

You don't have to apologize to me, Nikki. I was upset when I found out, because I think they should have told us. But I'm so thankful to know that you're alive.

"He can sound like a clock. He can tick, he can tock . . ."

Cindy had been at our house for half an hour and was still mostly focused on Abby. They were on their second board book.

From across the room, Dan caught my eye and gave me a small smile. When Cindy finished reading, Abby slid to the floor and then pulled herself up on the bed across the room, the one Dan and I had wrestled downstairs from the guest room to the living room so that my sister would not have to go up and down the stairs.

If only I knew Cindy well enough to read her expression. Was she in pain? Maybe seeing my daughter had made her sad, reminding her of her recent loss. I asked her a couple of times if she was okay, and each time she said she was all right. Still, her eyes looked slightly glazed, and she moved slowly, gingerly, in a way I doubted was usual for her.

I had always been incapable of schooling my features into a mask; my feelings were always clearly etched on my face. But Cindy's was still new, unfrozen from the photos I'd seen up to now. Her face was a story I couldn't yet read. I was struck by the notion that I'd encountered another version of myself, the person I might have been if I'd been raised by my first parents. But that was ridiculous, wasn't it? She was her own person.

When she looked at me, what did *she* see? Was I a kind of mirror for her as well—a glimpse of who she could have been, how she might have turned out if others had raised her?

Across the room, our husbands were obviously ready to pounce on any overlapping trait, no matter how insignificant. How could I blame them, really, when I was silently cataloguing all the similarities I could find? Still, I began to wish they would find something else to do as they looked from Cindy to me and back again, wearing matching grins.

"I've always wondered what it would be like to meet someone who was actually related to Nikki," Dan said to Cindy. "I thought I was prepared, but it's still so strange to see the two of you together."

Rick held up his camera and snapped our picture. Cindy frowned—it wasn't a quelling look, but it was clear she wished he had warned us. I was even less restrained, rolling my eyes before I could stop myself. "The paparazzi," I said, hoping for a laugh.

Rick tried to defend himself. "I *had* to! You should see your-selves. You both just tucked your hair behind your ear at the exact same time, the exact same way."

"How many different ways are there to do that?" Cindy asked, and I followed up: "You would do it, too, if you had long hair."

I didn't see Rick's reaction to being told off simultaneously by the two of us, though I heard Dan's snort from across the room. My eyes snapped back to my sister. We looked at each other, laughing with mutual recognition of the pressure to search for similarities that had not yet revealed themselves—or might not even exist—and the weight of this beyond-believable moment. As we sat side by side, giggling together, I thought, *Our voices may not sound alike, but our laughter does.*

On the second morning of Cindy's visit, I admitted how strange it felt to be someone else's biggest secret. I knew she understood secrets, especially the ones she'd been expected to keep for her family. "I'm glad you didn't stay a secret to me," she said.

We were sitting together at the round kitchen table Dan and I had bought in college, secondhand, for fifteen dollars. The kitchen curtains were open to the rain-soaked backyard, the woods behind our house. Droplets of water spattered the glass as my sister spoke about her childhood. Her eyes flitted to the window often, too—not, I thought, because she wanted to avoid looking at me, but only semiconsciously, as she pulled me along through her memories.

I already knew parts of the story. When Cindy was a baby, our parents and half sister, Jessica, moved to Seattle, and Cindy stayed behind with her maternal grandmother in Seoul. Partway through kindergarten, she reunited with her parents. "I couldn't even remember our mom," she said. "I just assumed that she loved me, that she had missed me. When I saw her again, I was so scared. I thought, 'Who is this angry woman? Is this really my mother?'"

Young, vulnerable, unsure of her place in the family she had not lived with for years, she made an easy target for our mother's frustration and rage. For years, she thought, *All parents must do this.* Our father either wasn't aware of how bad it was at first, working all the time and tutoring on the side, or didn't know how to stop it. Their aging grandmother wasn't able to protect her. Jessica, who was nearly ten years older than Cindy, was busy with work and school and rarely at home—she often complained about their family, but she had the ability to escape. As a teenager, Jessica was also big enough to grab their mother's arm when it was raised against her. Cindy was too young and too small to fight back, so their mother focused on her.

Gradually, Cindy realized that the way her mother treated her was *not* normal. She began to wish for a different life because hers made no sense to her. And even though our reasons were so different and she'd had the worst of it by far, this reminded me so poignantly of how I used to feel, too.

As a child, Cindy never got the other life she wanted, though a friend's mother did offer to take her in once—not because she knew the truth, but because she was kind and could see that Cindy was unhappy. "My parents would never have let me live with someone else. The shame, you know. They told me, all the time, 'Don't tell anyone what goes on in our family; it's not their business.'" She swiped at her eyes as we talked. At some point I had reached over, I wasn't sure when, to cover her hand with mine. I left it there, and listened.

I wanted to cry, too, for my sister now and also for the child she'd been. But I knew it took courage for her to share these things with me, and I wanted to be strong for her and not break down. It seemed the least I owed her, when I had escaped, and she had not.

Cindy had brought an old photo album with her, and she flipped through it with me, pointing out Jessica, our father, our maternal and paternal grandmothers, our aunts and uncles. She gave me a small stack of photos to keep. One of our father in an apartment in 1975. One of him and Cindy at her wedding reception in 2002. Jessica and Cindy shopping together at a mall, sometime in the 1990s.

And then there were the rare, precious photos from her childhood in Korea. Two round-cheeked girls with shining black hair and serious expressions: Jessica at twelve, and Cindy as a toddler. A picture of Cindy by herself, her face in profile, which made me smile more than any of the others—not just because I could see that, as little girls, side by side, we would have resembled each other more closely than we did now. A green sundress, her hair in pigtails, her long legs dangling from a park bench—I could see traces of the woman beside me in the girl's eyes: my sister, at the age of three, before our mother got a hold of her.

She had no pictures from the Seattle years, before or after our parents' divorce. No pictures of our mother at all. Jessica had emailed me a couple of photos of our mom, and I did not see the strong resemblance Cindy said she could see between us, but that might have been the age difference. There was something to the shape of our mother's face, the softness around her cheeks and the point of her chin, that did remind me of my own reflection.

"We weren't the kind of family that took portraits," Cindy said now. "Our parents spent most of their time working. When they were home, I just tried to stay out of their way."

Would it ever feel normal to hear my sister say the words *our parents*? Looking at Cindy's few childhood photos, my thoughts turned to my husband's relationship with his siblings, and how their common history had supplied them with a code, an understanding, unique to the three of them. They had grown up on the same island; the same people, stories, rituals, and rules, year in and year out, shaped each of them in turn and bound them together. Cindy and I would never have that kind of history. I would never know what it was like to grow up with her as my big sister, looking out for me.

Looking at little Cindy on the park bench, I wished I could magically insert myself in the photograph. I wished we had actual memories together, instead of years of secrets and silence. As I sat there, wanting the impossible, a question formed in my mind—one I had wanted to give voice to ever since I learned of her, one I still wasn't quite sure how to ask.

"Do you see the pretty butterfly, Abby?"

My sister was holding my daughter's hand, gazing at a small yellow-and-black butterfly resting on a dewy leaf. We had spent the first couple of days of their visit at our house, just talking, in part because Cindy still needed to rest. When she said she felt up to a little walking, we decided to visit the Museum of Life and Science. Abby was too young for most of the exhibits, but she was excited when we stopped in the butterfly house. She pulled her aunt by the hand, trying to follow one of the many hundreds of butterflies flitting through trees and vines and botanical flowers.

"She's really going to make Cindy want a baby," Rick said as we watched them.

Since he'd been the one to broach the topic, I mentioned Cindy had told me they were going to try again. I thought perhaps Rick would tell me to mind my own business, or clam up at least, but he didn't. I wondered if he was beginning to think of me as family, too.

Losing the pregnancy, he said, had been very difficult. But it had also made them realize how much they wanted to be parents.

"I hope it's not making it worse, seeing Abby."

"Not at all. Cindy is having a great time with her." Rick grinned. "When she found out about you *and* learned you were pregnant, she said it was like getting two for the price of one."

That evening, Rick made us his "famous meat loaf" for dinner, promising us German pancakes for breakfast the following day. "I like to cook and bake," he explained as he scribbled a grocery list.

"I do all the baking, actually, because Cindy never wants to read the directions. She's a great cook, but she can't follow a recipe."

"Don't you judge me," Cindy told him. "Recipes are tedious."

Another way we were different: I had always loved a good set of clear instructions. "So I can't ask you for your favorite Korean recipes, I guess?"

"No, but I can show you how to make them." I didn't want her to go to the Korean grocery or spend more time on her feet, cooking for all of us. "Next time," she agreed. We went out to a Korean restaurant instead, where we all ate bulgogi and I took pictures of Abby posing with her chopsticks arranged like elephant tusks. Cindy admitted that she loved when other people cooked for her— she'd often been responsible for making the meals, growing up with her dad and stepmom.

This reminded me that I'd wanted to talk with her in person about our father. Fair or not, she was my gateway into the family and, by extension, into his world. He and I had not yet met, though we kept in touch via email—the simplest means for both of us, given his self-consciousness about his (very good) English and my nonexistent Korean. I was beginning to think I would like to meet him.

When I asked questions, he didn't always react well. I'd gotten crumbs about the family, sometimes from him and sometimes from Cindy; I'd heard things like *Dad's parents were farmers in Korea* or *I think you take after Mom and Grandma, a little bit.* Once I asked my birth father what I thought was an innocent question, about the places he had lived and why he'd wanted to come to America. *Please don't ask me any more questions about the past,* he wrote back. *It's my personal life.* Horrified that I'd overstepped, I apologized, but of course I was still desperately curious. I feared alarming him, causing him to pull away from me entirely. I didn't want his letters to stop for good. So I kept mine light, conversational, and tried not to ask too many questions.

My birth father insisted he wanted to get to know me. But every communication seemed to remind him of the adoption, secrets long denied. Every time he wrote, would he feel the need to apologize for things for which I did not blame him? Adoption was normal for me in a way it wasn't for him, or even my sister. While my adoptive parents balked at discussing certain things—while they never seemed comfortable talking about our differences, or the people who had created me—adoption was never a dark, embarrassing secret in our family. I had a lifetime of experience grappling and trying to come to terms with my adoption, a huge head start on anyone in my birth family.

"I know he doesn't like to talk about the past," I said. "But that's the part I missed. I don't know what to talk to him about, if not that."

"He doesn't really talk about it with me, either. Every once in a while he'll tell me about someone, or share some story I've never heard before. But there is a lot I don't know."

I was sorry to hear it, but in a way I also felt a little better: it wasn't just me. If our father saw the past as none of my business, perhaps it wasn't because I'd been adopted or because he didn't think of me as his real daughter—perhaps that's just how he was.

"Dad is getting older," Cindy said. "He seems healthy. But if you're thinking about meeting him, asking him your questions in person . . . maybe don't wait too long."

Was it a narrowing window she referred to, or a door closing? She had told me that our father had not told anyone else in the family about me. Sometimes I doubted he ever would. As happy as he was to be in contact, to know I was alive, he would prefer them to think me dead than learn about the adoption. Cindy told me some of our relatives in Korea might be shocked, lord it over him if they knew the truth about my adoption. For this reason—to save face, she supposed—and also for others she could only guess at, I remained our family's biggest secret.

What might Cindy and I do with the decades we had left, now that we knew about each other? I hoped we would become close; visit each other often. I had let myself imagine taking a trip to Korea together. But even if we did, I wouldn't be able to meet our family. What would she do—introduce me as a "friend," hope our relatives there wouldn't see the resemblance? It seemed so ridiculous, yet I had to wonder if that lie was in our future.

I studied Cindy again, doubts encroaching on the hope I had felt when she arrived at my home and hugged me. If I was our father's unacknowledged, unknown child, what was I to Cindy, the legitimate daughter? *Was* I just a friend to her—someone she'd come to visit this once, someone to whom she would write, but not someone who would ever be family? Or were we on our way to being real sisters, despite our family's secrets and all the years we had spent apart?

T he first time I asked someone to be my sister, I was ten years old.

I was on the playground at school, sitting on my favorite swing, where I could watch some of the other kids playing kickball on the blacktop fifty feet away. I glanced over and there she was, a couple of swings over, a girl with long black braids, round glasses, a striped dress, and black patent-leather shoes. She was younger than me, I thought, by at least a year. Her head was turned toward the blacktop, too, as if she were wondering if it was all right to join the other kids.

For an instant, in my excitement, I forgot about everyone else. Her hair, I thought. Her eyes! She looked like me. Well, more like me than anyone else I'd ever met at school. "Are you new?" I blurted.

The braided pigtails bounced as she nodded.

I told her my name. Hers was Kaitlyn, and she was two years younger than me. I wondered if the kids in her class were nice to her.

After that, we often met by the swings. She would run up and find me, almost knocking me over with hugs. We found secret hiding places and exchanged handwritten, carefully folded notes to be unfurled and read later. We played hide-and-seek and hopscotch and jumped rope side by side. I stopped asking for library passes at recess.

I often went to my grandmother's house after school, as she lived not far from my elementary school and could easily pick me up when my parents were working. Grandma was a constant presence throughout my childhood; I spent countless weekends and vacations with her, learning how to plant a vegetable garden, roller-skate, bait a hook, can green beans and peaches, and pick out the most likely murderer on the weekly crime procedurals we both loved. We would go to the Oregon coast for weeks at a time every summer, where we slept in my grandparents' camper and played pinochle and caught Dungeness crabs in the choppy waters of the bay. Grandma and I were always close, and I listened and deferred to her in a way I didn't with anyone else in my life. One day after school, when I told her about my new friend, she said, "You should look out for her, Nicole. She's younger than you."

Grandma was always emphasizing the importance of responsibility; I had received the same direction on rare occasions when my younger cousins came to visit. But then she said something that surprised me: "Maybe you should ask her if she wants to be your sister. It's a very special thing to have a sister."

She reminded me that my mother and my aunt, who lived thousands of miles apart, would talk on the phone for hours. She told me again how much she had loved and relied on her late sister, Mary, who died before my parents adopted me. "Mary always looked out for me," she said. "All our lives! That's what sisters do. Maybe your friend needs someone to look out for her, too."

So one day I asked Kaitlyn, rather nervously, if she already had a sister, because I didn't want to take anyone else's rightful place. Kaitlyn said no. "I don't, either," I said. "Do you want to be my little sister, just when we're at school? Just for pretend?"

To my joy and relief, she smiled and said, "Sure!" Then she asked if she could come over to my house to play sometime. I'd never had a school friend over before; I promised I would ask my parents.

A few weeks later, I noticed she was absent for several days straight. Did she have the flu? The chicken pox? I wondered and worried for a week or so, then asked one of her classmates what was going on. "Kaitlyn doesn't go here anymore," she told me.

She and I had never exchanged our phone numbers; I had no way to reach her. I had no idea if she had moved away or simply transferred schools. I felt sure if she'd known ahead of time, she would have warned me. Or maybe she just hadn't known how to tell me? On my way in from recess I threw out a note I'd been holding for days, shifting from pocket to pocket, hoping for a chance to hand over to her.

The next day, I asked my teacher for a library pass at recess.

One night during her visit, Cindy caught me absently writing on my dinner place mat. Not with a pen, but with a fingertip: up and down, across the edge of the mat, invisible letters I could almost see in my mind's eye. When she commented on it, I explained, a little sheepishly, that the note-taking was a lifelong habit. It happened when I was talking with or listening to people—sometimes intentionally, the words related to our conversation, but usually without even realizing it.

"Our dad does that all the time! Sometimes he writes in English, sometimes in Korean. I do it, too. I always thought I picked up the habit from watching him."

"Maybe not," Dan said.

Laughing, we began to muse about whether there was a "writing with no paper" gene. The invisible writing on any nearby surface was a habit that had been good-naturedly mocked by friends and family for as long as I could remember. People had remarked upon how strange they thought it was. My boss at my first job, back in high school, had called it "distracting." Now it was something more, too: another little link between Cindy and me, and to our father the writer.

After dinner, Cindy and I went for a walk while Dan and Rick cleaned up. Cindy joked about what devoted spouses they were for taking care of the chores and giving us more time to talk, but I was too busy thinking about the question that had been weighing on my mind, the question I still hadn't asked.

We were as closely related as people could be, products of the same parents but with vastly different homes and lives. There had been no reason to expect that our personalities would mesh, that our lives would fit together like pieces of the same puzzle just because I might want them to. I had tried so hard to manage my expectations leading up to this visit. But my hopes were another matter entirely. I wanted so much of Cindy—what if it was too much?

She would be going home in just a few days. My chest felt tight. I remembered something Rick had said to me once, right after I got in touch with Cindy: *In her own way, she was as alone as you were.* Maybe some part of her needed me, too? Anxious as I was, I knew this moment, this one request, was so important. And I was running out of time.

"I really don't know how to be a sister, because I've never been one before." I was talking too fast; my words tumbled out in a rush, as if someone else were pulling them from my throat. "I know that you aren't used to expecting much from your family. But I want you to expect things from me. I want you to feel like you can trust me and tell me things, and know that I will support you."

I felt Cindy's eyes and stopped. Stopped talking, stopped walking, right in the middle of the darkened, rain-drenched street. She tilted her head and pursed her lips ever so slightly, assuming a thoughtful expression that was—like so many of her mannerisms—eerily familiar.

I closed my eyes and took a deep breath, determined to salvage the conversation, reassure her that I wasn't as desperate as I felt. It had come out all wrong. Too fast, too sudden, too much.

"I know it will take a while, and that's okay; I can be patient. I just want you to know—because I hope we'll always be honest with each other—that that's the kind of relationship I want to have some-day. I want us to be real sisters. Do you . . . do you think we could get there, someday?"

I could barely discern Cindy's expression in the dim light cast by streetlamps, even if I'd had more practice at reading her face. She didn't seem to pick up on my emotion, how afraid I was that she would refuse. She reached out and took my hand, her fingers strong and warm, squeezing mine tightly.

"You're already there with me, Nikki."

She smiled, and I did, too, the darkness hiding my tears. The two of us circled the block two more times. We must have kept talking, but later I would never remember exactly what we said. All I could think about, the whole time, was how happy I was.

I still wasn't sure if my birth parents were glad I had found them. I still didn't know if or when I would meet them, or what to think about their decision to give me up. But I believed Cindy when she said that she wanted us to be family—real sisters—because in the time we had known each other, she had offered me nothing except for the truth. I knew that she'd been alone, too, probably more alone than I was. I could just believe that maybe she needed me as much as I needed her.

Though we'd forged a different bond than siblings who grew up together, it was, I now understood, no less important for being so new. It didn't matter how different we were, how much we had missed, how long we'd been apart. We had been family once, and now we would be again. We were sisters, at last, because we had decided we should be.

Part IV

C indy called me on March 12, almost one year to the day since we met. "I'm pregnant again."

I willed myself not to shout with joy, even though I wanted to. I understood why my sister's voice was more cautious than thrilled. In the year since her ectopic pregnancy and surgery, she'd also had a miscarriage. "If it happens again," she had told me a few months earlier, "I don't know if I'll be up for another try."

Now she said she was about six weeks along. "We haven't told anyone else."

"Not even your dad?"

I still never referred to him as my dad. Rick had suggested Abeoji, *Father* in Korean, because that's what he called my birth father. For me, though, it didn't make a difference whether the word was in Korean or English; the meaning was the same, and even if *Father* or *Dad* had felt right to *me*, I did not know if my birth father would agree. Harabeoji could be used for a respected elder, not necessarily a grandparent, but that, too, felt wrong—he *was* my biological father, not a more distant connection. In emails, I addressed him by his first name and just felt awkward about it, as if it were disrespectful, but he never asked me to do otherwise.

"No, I'm not going to tell him until my second trimester, if I make it that far," Cindy said. "For now, you're the only one who knows."

I heard the fear in her voice and wished she had no reason for it. I wished this pregnancy could be something we laughed and joked about, even this early.

"I'm trying not to obsess over it," she added. "Every day feels like a victory, though. Another bridge between me and this baby."

For now, as my sister waited and worried, I decided not to mention our decision to try to have another baby—I could wait until she was safely in her second trimester. "I'm thinking about you both," I said, wishing I could hug her instead.

We both knew that the fate of this pregnancy had no connection to my thoughts, our wishes, or anyone's prayers. But she was my sister, and she wanted this so badly. I hoped for her as hard as I dared, knowing a part of her was still afraid to hope for herself.

I did get pregnant, too, confirmed by the test I took three days after my twenty-ninth birthday. By the time I shared the news with Cindy—sending her a video of Abby announcing, "I'm going to be a big sister!"—my sister was in her second trimester and feeling optimistic. Thrilled to be pregnant at the same time, our phone conversations were filled with talk about cousins and favorite name combinations. Abby, by then a precocious and highly chatty two-year-old, was certain both babies would be girls.

Dan and I had booked July flights to visit Cindy and Rick before I learned I was pregnant. "The trip won't be a problem," I assured my sister. "Can you just make sure your freezer is well-stocked with popsicles? I can't be pregnant without popsicles."

"That's not a problem. By the way, I've been wanting to ask . . .

would you like Dad to come and stay with us for a couple of days while you're here, so you can meet him, too?"

I didn't say yes right away.

Wasn't this what I had wanted, envisioned when I searched—the chance to meet and talk with a biological parent? As much as I loved my sister, as close as we'd become, I had not gotten my looks, my traits, my flesh and blood and bone from her. We were stems that shared common roots, but there were some things I simply could not know unless I met one or both birth parents. I'd given up on forging a deeper connection with my birth mother. But I was willing to meet my birth father, and assumed I *would* one day. The meeting would likely have already taken place if we lived on the same coast.

"Was this his idea, or yours?" I wasn't sure why this mattered, but it did. I didn't want to frighten him, or force him into a meeting he didn't want.

"I told him you would be here, but he's the one who asked if you would like to meet."

He and his wife had offered to come and spend a couple of days with us at Cindy's house. They wouldn't stay the whole week—Cindy wanted to be sure that she and I still got plenty of time together. "I know that he would like to see you, but you can say no," she said. "He'll understand if you're not ready. But he is. It's what he wants."

I did feel ready, in a way. I might not be ready to stay with him, or have him stay with me, for long—but visiting with him at my sister's house, with her there for support, sounded like the easiest possible introduction.

Yet if I'd once worried that I would disappoint Cindy, it was nothing compared to how much I feared disappointing our father. He and I came from different generations, different cultures, different traumas. I was not the person I would have been if he had raised me. And I was not a good Korean daughter, obedient and respectful, like my sister had been right up until she learned about me and shook off a lifetime's worth of conditioning to demand answers—if I had once feared alienating her with my bluntness and outspokenness, what chance would I have when I met our father? Sometimes, when he closed himself off from questions, or reiterated that he didn't want anyone else in the family to know about me, I still feared he was ashamed of me. Or, if not me, at least the history I represented.

But I did not want to continue going to visit my sister regularly, ignoring my father's requests to meet. I did not want to be estranged from both my birth parents forever.

"It's going to be weird," I said. It wasn't a refusal to meet, or an argument against it, just a fact.

"*Super* weird," my sister agreed. "But this is our family we're talking about. What else could it be?"

Dan, Abigail, and I landed in Portland on July 9. My birth father and his wife were due to arrive the following afternoon. I was, as I had known I would be, in the depths of early pregnancy fatigue, worn out and cranky after ten hours of travel with a toddler. I had expected a night of poor sleep in my sister's guest bed, but my anxiety over meeting my birth father was no match for first-trimester exhaustion. At least I was prepared for it this time, and past the worst of my nausea.

The next morning I was the last to rise. While I ate breakfast, Cindy asked if we wanted to go to Multnomah Falls. I had not been there since childhood, and the promised short hike and lovely views seemed far preferable to sitting in my sister's living room, staring at the clock while we waited for our father. As we walked over trails and damp bridges, Abby often riding on Dan's shoulders, the sun broke through the hazy cloud cover above, making the waterfall gleam silver amid all the green. At Abby's request we bought hot dogs and ice cream cones from the snack bar and sat near the base of the falls while we ate, listening to the water cascading behind us.

Either Dan or Rick took a spectacularly bad picture of my sister and me with our arms around each other's shoulders, both our faces rounded by pregnancy. *We look so alike in this one,* I thought as I looked at the photo, the two of us half smiling and squinting in the sun, strands of black hair escaping from matching ponytails.

As we drove back to Cindy and Rick's house, Abby nodding off in her car seat, I fell silent. The whole car was quiet. Rick and I tended to carry the small talk when the four of us were all together. I felt like I did before an important interview, or the first day of school, wondering if people would like me. Worried about the impression I'd made. "Dad told me that he's nervous, too," Cindy said.

This did not make me feel better. "What if we're both so nervous we don't have anything to say?"

"Well, then, you can just stare at each other for a while, and then we'll eat delicious Korean food."

I was so grateful, so glad she was with me for this meeting. Sometimes I tried to imagine reuniting with my birth family with no Cindy in the picture. How would it have gone? Would I have ever met my birth father? Even if I hadn't, everything I'd gone through to find my family would have been worth it, I thought, as long as I ended up with this woman beside me.

"You don't need to worry, Nikki," she said. "I know he's happy that the two of you are finally going to meet. Just . . . don't be too offended by anything he says, okay?" I think she meant to smile, but it looked more like a grimace. "I meant to warn you before—I think sometimes Koreans can be really blunt."

I didn't want our father to be blunt with me—not right after we met—unless it resulted in untrammeled praise. His emails to me were kind enough, but also brief. I still didn't know how he truly felt about me. What did it mean if your own father didn't like you?

"What if he's disappointed?" I said in a low voice, meant only for my sister. "What if he thinks I should be . . . you know, more Korean?"

I was glad she didn't laugh, though I thought I saw a glimmer of mischief in her eyes as she replied, "Then I think you can tell him he knows perfectly well why you're not."

Back at the house, I didn't even have time to take off my shoes or fix my mussed ponytail before the doorbell rang. Rick did an about-face. "They're early! Usually they're late because they get lost. Family trait," he added, grinning at me. "You all have a poor sense of direction." I would have liked to throw something at him, but I knew he was right.

He opened the door. My birth father and his wife stood on the porch, their arms full of luggage, gift bags, and two enormous containers of marinating meat I imagined I could smell even through the Tupperware. *He looks so much like Cindy*, I thought.

In appearance, my sister truly was a younger, female version of our father—something I had not fully seen until this moment, despite all the photos. They had the same eyes, though his were sharp behind his glasses and I was more accustomed to seeing my sister with her contacts in. They had the same nose, the same freckles. Their faces were shaped the same as well, not as round or full as mine, both concealing more than my wide-open book of a face. I'd known that they looked alike, of course, from photos, but the resemblance was so much more striking in person—and it seemed fitting that the daughter who'd grown up under his eye looked more like him than the one he'd never had a chance to know. *I must look like our mother*, I thought. And then I wished I didn't, in case it gave him another reason not to like me.

I had scrutinized his dark eyes and stern mouth in photographs, unable to find any real resemblance between us. But in person, there was something familiar in the determined set of his chin, the quick movement of his eyes that seemed so familiar. He held himself like someone with discipline. I knew myself to *be* disciplined, but probably did not appear so to others. He moved with purpose and care, like Cindy, and when he halted in front of me he seemed to size me up. I wondered if his mind was churning as fast as mine. I was conscious of straightening my spine, trying to meet his gaze without fear. He was only an inch taller than me. He should not have seemed so imposing, this trim, fit Korean man nearing seventy.

But I felt small in his presence. And so very, very young.

"Hello, Nikki," he said.

"Hello," I said, leaving off both the uncomfortable *Dad* and the unthinkable *Mr. Chung*, still too nervous to smile. I envied his oh-so-easy use of my old nickname as he held out his hand. Our handshake seemed too formal, even if I wasn't sure I wanted to hug him yet.

"You're looking very plump."

"I'm *pregnant*," I reminded him, my voice a shadow of what it would have been if one of my adoptive parents had said that to me. "Thirteen weeks."

His wife, who immediately hugged me as if I were her own long-lost daughter and not only her husband's, nodded at my sister. "You look the same size as Cindy, but she is much farther along than you."

I looked at my sister. First her stomach, then her face. *I warned you*, her raised eyebrows seemed to say. "It's my second pregnancy. You start to show earlier," I said. For some reason, our absurd exchange made me think of my birth mother, who Cindy had said never showed even when she was several months along—already, I felt, I was not measuring up to expectations.

For a few moments, we all bustled about, finding places for bags and luggage. Rick kept asking questions that were sometimes answered in Korean; Cindy would translate. Would every exchange we had be like this? My sister explaining what our father had said to me? Even if he spoke in English—which he spoke very well—were there nuances, inferences, cultural references I would miss unless Cindy drew my attention to them?

Stomach in knots again, I was seized by the desire to flee. I didn't know what I was doing here, or why I'd thought this meeting was a good idea. I should have waited. I should have given us more time. He was going to be disappointed in me, I was sure of it, if he wasn't already. I was jet-lagged, pregnant, still slightly sweaty from hiking, and now distracted by my daughter, who was very loudly requesting a snack.

As it turned out, Abigail saved me, cranky or not; Cindy's stepmother had swooped down on her, giving her the biggest Minnie Mouse doll I had ever seen. I was grateful for the moment of distraction, the chance to shore myself up as Abby was given her first Korean lesson: *Kamsahamnida, Halmeoni, Harabeoji.* That much even I knew.

"We brought you something, too," my birth father said. He gave Cindy and me copies of *Walden* and *Civil Disobedience.* "Have you read this?"

"Um," I said. "Not since high school."

"You can both read, and then we can discuss it."

Yes, I thought. *Transcendentalist family book club. All very normal.*

Then he handed me a copy of the book of essays he'd written. When I reconnected with my birth family, I had been surprised to learn that my sister wrote poems and stories in her free time, while our father was a published author, a lover of language, and a scholar of Korean literature and linguistics. My own lifelong obsession with writing was a shared family trait, the inheritance of what I was told were generations of scholars and writers.

I wished I could read his essays. I was sure I would understand so much more about him if I could. But they were written in Korean, as inaccessible to me as the man himself had once been. I turned to the cover page and saw that he had written an inscription in English. I thanked him, happy all the same to be holding a book filled with his words, signed with his love and prayers, even though we both knew that his note was the only part I would be able to read.

Dan excused himself to wrangle Abby napwards. I could tell that my birth father and his wife already liked my daughter and would have been glad for her to stay, but she was still worn out from the flight the day before and now hours overdue for a nap, her mood fraying at the edges. Rick also disappeared upstairs, taking his in-laws' luggage with him. Left alone—intentionally, I suspected—my birth father and I sat on one couch, while Cindy and her stepmother sat on the other. Watching her stepmom reach over to cover Cindy's hand in a silent gesture of affection, I remembered she was more of a mother to my sister than her own had been.

I pulled out the album of pictures I'd brought, stuffed with photos traversing the years between infancy and my college graduation. My birth father and his wife both leaned over to look, holding themselves so still, listening while I narrated. "This is my mom and my dad," I began, pointing to pictures of my parents holding me just days after they had brought me home. They both looked so happy, almost in disbelief, all wide smiles while I dozed on them in my premie-sized strawberry dress.

I hesitated as I said the words *mom* and *dad*, wondering if my birth father had noticed. Here he was, meeting his adult child for the first time, seeing pictures of a childhood he had missed and the white strangers who had raised her. It had to be as unsettling for him as it was for me. I wished I could say something comforting to him, but what?

I had told him so many times that I did not hold my adoption against him. But even two years after our first correspondence, his letters to me were filled with regret. He held it against himself, and I did not want him to. How strange, yet not strange at all, that I felt the same urge to protect him that I'd felt toward my adoptive parents. Perhaps it was a sign of how much I already cared about him. Was there some magical, inspired phrase I could snatch out of the stifled air between us, something I could say that would make him lay his guilt to rest, once and for all?

As we flipped through my pictures, I could tell that he was doing his best to listen and contribute to the conversation. At times the other three would lapse into Korean, and then one of them, usually

Cindy or our father, would translate. Sometimes they apologized, but I felt no annoyance; only embarrassment at my own inability to understand the language I had been born to speak. I'd been cut off from my culture of origin, yes, but that had been decades ago; I'd had almost thirty years to ask questions, to try to learn more about it. The gap between us wasn't just his to bridge, and yet I'd come without any real tools.

As we looked at pictures from my commencement, my grinning in a black robe and honor cords while my mom smiled proudly and my dad held my diploma tube aloft, my birth father told me how proud he was of me "for graduating from one of the best colleges in the world." I turned the page, and there were a handful of wedding snapshots: Dan and me in one of them; another of me flanked by my parents. Since I'd learned about him, I had often wondered if my father would think of my quiet life of writing and editing at the margins. I was still thinking about graduate school, harboring dreams of becoming a writer, but had spent most of my time home with Abby ever since I'd been laid off following my maternity leave. Had my birth father hoped I would do more with my life? Wouldn't a string of impressive accomplishments make his sacrifice seem more worthwhile?

As Rick would later point out, when he saw me last I had been a two-pound infant whose survival was far from certain. Based on what the doctors must have told him, I might have surpassed his expectations just by living. By thriving. "It must seem like a miracle to him," my atheist brother-in-law told me.

When we had looked through all of my photos, they showed me their own family albums. I felt so nosy in my eagerness, asking so many questions they could hardly keep up, but I wanted so badly to know who everyone was, how I was related to them. My birth father told me about his deceased parents, to whom he'd been close—though he was not the eldest, he was the smartest, and they did what they could to help him further the education he wanted so much. He also told me about his brother and sisters in Korea, and showed me photographs of them. I wished I could meet them some-day, though I knew it was unlikely.

I was most intrigued when he mentioned the ten volumes of fam-ily history in his elder brother's library in Korea. Our oldest known ancestor had lived more than five hundred years ago, and our fa-ther and his siblings were of the seventeenth generation since. As an adoptee, I had never been part of such a lineage, generations stitched together through time and recorded memory. The common stories, the shared mannerisms, the physical traits linking one relative to another in a multigenerational tapestry—I had never known these particular aspects of family, of belonging. When I heard family sto-ries growing up, I was always reminded that I had been grafted onto the family tree; I had never been of it, part of it, the way my other relatives were.

I wondered if nonadopted people could possibly appreciate what an unimaginable gift it was to possess such a history—the history my birth father apparently took for granted, recorded and preserved through the long generations. Who knew how the fam-ily book had been edited, facts suppressed or rewritten over the years—but it would still be a marvel to have that kind of legacy at my fingertips. What might those volumes spanning the centuries re-veal, if I were able to read them? What might fall out as I turned the pages—sepia-toned photographs or hand-drawn portraits; dusty certificates announcing marriages or births?

I had never been a part of any of it. Yet just knowing that it ex-isted made me feel connected, in some small way, to all the people who came before me. Of course, I would not have expected to be in the book, as Cindy was; you can't keep your secret daughter a secret if you write her name in the family book. Theirs was an entire world I was not a part of, and so learning that I was—of course—omitted from the official family history did not surprise me.

As far as losses went, it was small compared to the loss of a parent, a sister, a language, a culture. But it did make me wonder ex-actly what and who had also been left out, forgotten, in the eighteen known generations of the family. *Nineteen*, I amended, thinking of Abby and her little sibling, and my sister's baby on the way.

"Do you think I look like anyone in your family?" I asked.

With every question, every word, I feared my father would think I was asking too much, but he looked at me carefully, as if trying to read my face the way I'd tried to read his. "My mother, maybe, a little bit. You look a lot like Cindy, too."

He said that he had chosen my Korean name, Soo Jung, before I was born. As it happened, the name Susan—the one on my original birth certificate, the one in my long-sealed adoption file—was chosen because it shared a first syllable with my Korean name, hitting the ear in a similar fashion. Cindy's name was In Jong; in Korean, the second syllable of our names was the same. I watched our father's finger fly in the air, tracing it out, and the movement reminded me of the day Cindy had caught me writing invisible words on my place mat.

My sister would later tell me how surprised she was by how much our father talked during our visit. And he was talking to *us*—not only to me. He included Cindy, sometimes asking her questions in English or Korean about what she remembered. He told us things that made us sad, and also things that made us laugh—like how his lifelong sweet tooth developed when occupying soldiers gave him candy from their rations and care packages. Talking about the past clearly wasn't easy, and both his own private nature and cultural conditioning should have made it challenging to defer to his daughters. Yet we could tell he was trying to do just that, all through the visit. He opened doors for us, cooked and served us dinner, fell silent when we spoke in order to listen. He answered all our questions, sharing what he remembered even when it was painful.

"Every word, every action, even his body language and manner of address was like an apology—to both you and Cindy," Rick said afterward. "He was humbling himself."

Sitting next to my father, listening to him speak, I felt sure that many of the things my adoptive family had always found puzzling—

my studiousness, my freakish memory, my wide perfectionist streak—would have seemed natural to him. I thought again of my mother's comment, long ago: "We weren't prepared to raise a child like you." When I asked what she meant, she did not mention my precociousness or my nonstop questions or my reading and scribbling in journals, but perhaps she was thinking of all those things when she said, "You were just really intense, and always surprising us."

Who might I have been if my birth father had been the one to raise me? Even without his influence in my life, he had managed to pass things on. I considered his writing, his obvious pride in it and in his past scholarship. These seemed to be the essence of his identity, these passions that had never been his whole career—things he'd made time for at the edges of a life more focused on practical matters, hard work, survival. Whatever else he was, he was a student and a writer first. No, I would not have surprised him.

He was the one to bring up my birth mother. "When she became pregnant with you, she said she didn't want another girl," he said. Simply, calmly, without anger, but with a shake of the head as if to suggest he still couldn't understand it. I nodded: I knew this already; he had told me before. But hearing the words in his voice made them seem more real.

"I knew how she treated Cindy, and I thought to myself, this woman cannot have a baby. Then you were born so early. I thought adoption was the only way. I didn't know what else to do."

His voice shook when he told me about visiting the NICU, seeing me in the incubator. "I went one time," he admitted. I did not ask him why it was only once; I guessed it was because it was too hard to see me, as small and sick as I was, and he knew that soon I would not be his daughter to raise.

"You were so tiny, you fit in my hand, right in the palm of my hand!" He held out his hand, upturned, lined but still strong and firm, staring at it while he spoke—as if he could still make out the shape of a too-small baby in the curve of his palm. "I remember I was crying and crying," he said, and then he was crying again.

Cindy had told me when she confronted him about the adoption, the secrets and omissions, he insisted that he had put me out of his thoughts. He thought I'd gone on to have a good life. He'd provided for me, in a sense, and had no choice but to move on. He claimed he had *forgotten* the adoption, for a time, and that's why he denied it.

I still didn't understand, not entirely. But I was moved to know that no matter how hard he may have tried, he *hadn't* entirely forgotten about me after I was gone, adopted and beyond reach. He had retained this one memory of me from the hospital, and it meant something to him.

I meant something to him.

I wished we were close enough for me to take his hand. I wanted to fill it with mine, to banish the memory of a sick, tiny infant and replace it with a new one: his grown daughter, strong enough to comfort him.

"I didn't know if you were going to be okay," he said.

He waved his hand at me, not in greeting this time, or acknowledgment, but as if to say, *See? You were okay.*

I nodded, my throat tight. *I am.*

On our last morning together, we all went to breakfast at a diner owned by a Korean family. We ate pajeon, savory Korean pancakes, and Abby got American-style Minnie Mouse pancakes drenched in syrup. Everyone fussed over her, offering her more food, and she reveled in being the center of attention.

After we ate, Rick suggested a local Catholic shrine set on several acres of gardens, as a nice place to walk around and take some family photos before my birth father and his wife began their journey home. The National Sanctuary to Our Sorrowful Mother, he and I knew it as "the Grotto." Like me, Rick had been raised Catholic, and both of us had childhood memories of the shrine—though he'd been there countless times, and I had visited only once, with my adoptive parents. I remembered the outdoor Stations of the Cross, and the gift shop where my mother bought me a Rosary of shiny green stones.

Sometimes my childhood faith had felt like my only culture, the one thing that had made me feel I was part of something larger. Now, standing in a chapel to Our Lady carved out of rock, Dan and Rick snapped several photos of Cindy and me with our father a short distance from a replica of Michelangelo's *Pietà*. I thought of the real *Pietà*, which Dan and I had seen in Rome years ago, and the statues of Mary and Joseph that had stood on the dresser in my childhood bedroom. My Korean family spoke a language I couldn't and shared a history of which I had never been a part, but here, surrounded by signs and symbols of my adopted faith, I was the one who felt most at home. Everyone watched me light a candle, one among rows of flickering votives, each one representing a prayer. As I recited a silent Hail Mary, I thought about two healthy babies, their names and their lives still unknown, part of the nineteenth generation since their oldest ancestor.

When it was time for them to leave, Cindy's parents hugged her and her family goodbye. My father's wife hugged me, too, before reaching into her purse to hand me an envelope. "Buy something for the baby," she said.

I tried to tell her—tell them both—that it was unnecessary, but there was no refusing. "They don't know what you need. They don't want you to leave empty-handed," Cindy whispered. I understood that giving back the money would be seen as a rejection—of the gift, and also of them; of whatever it was we now were to one another. So I thanked them, pocketing the cash, and promised to put it to good use.

My father's wife kissed my cheek, squeezing my hands just as she had squeezed my sister's, and then patted my stomach. I felt such a rush of affection for her—and gratitude for the love she'd shown Cindy. My father shook Dan's hand, touched Abby's cheek gently, and then turned to me. I was glad that he didn't try to shake my hand this time. He embraced me, and it felt right.

When he stepped back, I saw that he was smiling. It occurred to me that I had not seen him smile much during our visit. I didn't think he'd been unhappy—he seemed very happy indeed, if sometimes overwhelmed. Perhaps he really had been as nervous as I was, and his smile meant that he wasn't anymore.

"Come and visit us someday," he said to me. "We will be praying for you and your baby."

He was a God-fearing man, I knew. Like my adoptive parents, he really would pray for us. I had no idea if their combined intercessions would make a difference. But they were all my parents, in vastly different ways, and I was glad to have their prayers.

My father and I parted unsure of what we were, what we would be, to each other. I did not feel like a reclaimed daughter. It would be years before he would offer to tell any of his siblings about me, and then only one of them. To most of my birth family, I remain and may forever be a secret.

Yet I didn't watch him leave after our initial visit with a feeling of incompleteness, or dissatisfaction. I knew how much the handful of days in my company had cost him, not because he was unhappy to meet me, but because he had forced himself to be so open and vulnerable to someone who was still, essentially, a stranger. He wrote to me soon after our reunion, letting me know how much it had meant to him. At his request, I shared some of my writing with him, including an essay I'd written about my decision to search. He read it and responded kindly, without any criticism. He told me I took after him in my writing. He told me, again, that he was proud of me. It was almost enough.

> *It was an unforgettable meeting with you and Cindy. I was a little bit nervous and felt guilty. You were so special and nice to all of us with your understanding and love. It was just like a beautiful dream to see you last week. I pray every day for you and your baby as well as Cindy's.*

Most of my childhood assumptions about my biological parents now seem as foreign to me as the Korean culture I grew up without. But my father's belief that adoption was truly the best option in a sea of imperfect ones is something of which I am now certain. I believe it was the only thing he thought he could do for me—perhaps even the most loving thing. An amended version of the guesswork from my adoptive parents, I suppose that is still what I want to believe, in some form; the power of the narrative I'd grown up hearing may never entirely loosen its hold over me. In my birth father's case, I think the myth might actually be true: I remember it every time he expresses the old belief in his guilt, because I don't think it would affect him so much if he had not cared. When I consider the depths of that emotion, long buried but still present in him, I believe in his intention to ensure I was safe.

Still, when we finally met face-to-face at my sister's house, I wish I'd been brave enough to ask him just one more question. *Did* you *want to keep me?* Not *Did you see me as your responsibility?* Not *Would you have kept me if things had been different?*—but *Did* you *want me?*

It was the question that had hung over my every childhood thought about my birth family. It was the question that mattered most. My birth mother had answered it, once, in her way, though I still didn't know if I believed her. If I had asked my birth father, what would he have said?

In a way, I tried to answer it myself, by taking my unknown birth parents' love for granted all those years. Maybe believing that I had their love and regard functioned much the same as having it, being assured of it, would have. The belief that I'd actually been wanted from the beginning, paired with the sure knowledge that my adoptive parents loved me, allowed me to grasp at self-worth, despite my doubts; to grow up and live my life free of the darkest feelings of abandonment.

But for all my birth father's kindness, for all his humanity and moving humility, in the end I simply couldn't bring myself to ask if he had wanted to keep me. To ask would be to know, and I didn't want to have to live with the answer if it was no. Though he and I have seen each other, had other conversations since, it remains the one question I have never found the courage to ask.

For a long time, Abby clearly remembered our first meeting with my birth father and his wife, though now that she is older that memory has faded. She knows that they gave her gifts; she and her little sister, Grace, have seen them in person and in pictures since. She knows my adoptive parents, and Dan's parents, and understands that in a way she has three sets of grandparents, not the usual two.

She is also beginning to understand my adoption, in the words and the stories I've given her. She was barely four years old the first time she asked me, "Mama, what does 'adopted' mean?"

Her question and her steady, inquisitive eyes pulled me away from a grad school assignment. She must have heard me say the word in conversation, one of many times I'd assumed she wasn't listening, and waited to question me. And at first I was grateful to be ready with an answer, one I had formed with my own children in mind years before either of them were born.

"If you're adopted, like me, it means you need someone to be your mama or daddy, and someone else wants to take care of you and be your parent," I said. "So instead of being born to my parents,

I was born to other parents first, and then Grandma and Grandpa took care of me."

As I watched her frown, I began to doubt whether my carefully worded definition made sense to her. It had seemed as good a place as any to begin, but was she, after all, too young to hear it or understand? Until this moment, I doubted if she had ever so much as imagined that a parent might not keep their child. Somehow, in all the times I'd pictured having this conversation, I had never thought about how strange or frightening even the simplest definition of adoption might sound to a child.

"Am I going to be adopted, too?" she asked.

"No! Most kids, like you, live with the parents they were born to. You will always be mine and Daddy's."

"I bet you liked your first mama best," she said, not realizing how much these words devastated me, "because Gracie and I like you the best."

I hesitated. Words I'd once heard from a birth mother flashed in my mind: *If there's something that everyone should know about adoption, it's that there is no end to this. There's no closure.* Now, more than ever, I knew that was true. Everything I had learned would have to be reexamined, relearned, and handed on to my children. Abby would have to know about my birth mother one day. She would learn that I had spoken with her on the phone. She would know why Cindy wasn't in contact with her.

My sister, of course, never told me I should choose sides. One day, many years after we met, she would confess that sometimes she still felt guilty for telling me the truth. "If I hadn't, then maybe you would have reached out to our mom. Maybe you would have had a relationship with her."

But whenever I tried to imagine Cindy hiding what really happened to her for my sake, it struck me as unbearably sad: how could we have gotten to know each other; grown as close as we have, with this secret between us? Eventually, I would have asked why she never talked to our mom, and what could she have said? She never asked me to choose; she never would. *I* felt I had to make a choice. I'd choose her, every time.

"I don't remember my first mother, so I don't really miss her," I finally told Abby, knowing she was too young to know everything. What I gave her was almost the truth. It was the only thing I felt ready to tell her about the one grandparent she'll never know. Though I still have not told my own daughters the full truth about the woman who bore me, I'm sure that—with my sister's help—I will tell them one day.

Since our first conversation, Abby has often asked what it was like for me, growing up adopted. Each time she aims her questions at different aspects of the experience: being Korean in a white family, being Korean when I didn't know any other Koreans, not knowing the people I'd come from, not having anyone I could ask. She knows I was probably better off for being adopted, though she doesn't yet know all the reasons, but she does think of it as hard. One time she told me it made her sad for me. I have never told her not to think of it that way—to be separated from your first family when you are too young to remember *is* a loss. That my deeply empathic, thoughtful older child is aware of that no longer surprises me.

Of course, plenty of adoptees don't think about their adoptions as much as I do. And many don't think about or dwell on the possible losses. When fellow adoptees tell me they don't really think about their birth parents, about being adopted at all, I believe them. All the same, my adoption no longer feels like mine alone to wonder about, or not—if it ever was. It is part of my sister's legacy, and our children's, too. So I don't try to convince my daughter that the way I lost one family and entered into a new one is entirely natural, that it was an uncomplicated happy event. It *was* happy, in a way, but it has also been a source of grief for many. It meant years of wondering and confusion for me; for her, it means she will know less about Korean culture than many other Korean kids whose parents were not adopted. It's okay if she sometimes feels sad when she thinks about that, about everything we've lost.

There are many different kinds of inheritances, many things we pass on, and adoption is only one of ours. If my children and my niece have a more complicated family history than some do, they also have a wonderful story to learn and tell someday. Another adoptee I know who has children—children who, like mine, have always known both their birth and adoptive relatives—once told me that, for all its challenges and surprises, she'll never take her family for granted. "Creating a home for my own children, seeing their absolute love for this family we've made, I always think: *Is this a dream? When am I going to wake up?*"

Over the years, I have heard more than one adopted person say, "We adoptees have a way of finding one another." I believe this is true—and to this day, it's always a welcome relief to find myself in the company of other adopted people, because only we can understand what it means to grow up adopted. To navigate our adoptive families, and our birth families, too, if we are privileged to know them, and build an identity from what has been lost and found.

Yet I've also found common ground sharing my story with people who, while not adopted, have distant or absent parents. Some of them, too, seek reconnection and reunion, with complicated results. A year or two after I met my birth father, I became friends with a woman who had grown up without her father, only to look for him as an adult. She seemed to understand and relate to my story as much as a fellow adoptee might.

Some of my friends who come from difficult or estranged families, who have lost and regained biological connections, wonder, as I do, whether our own kids will ever truly grasp what it was like for us growing up. While many of us earnestly try to share our truths and our memories with our children, because it is part of sharing our whole selves with them, it's not always easy to find the words. When my girls were younger, an adoption counselor told me that the most important thing is creating a culture of openness within the family, in which hard questions are never off-limits. "They should know they can ask you anything they want about the past, even if the answer is 'I will tell you when you're older,'" she said. "And then you have to follow through on that promise."

As our children have gotten older, Cindy and I have talked with greater intensity about when and how we will tell our daughters the whole truth about our family. We agree that it is their history to know one day; we have no interest in withholding it. And from a lifetime of questions, ones I often pondered all on my own, I know that one question will always lead to another and to another.

A few days before the first Christmas my sister and I were ever able to spend together, we stopped in at a neighborhood wine bar. Before ringing up our beer, wine, and the hard blackberry cider I persuaded my sister to try, the owner asked to see my ID. "Good genes!" she said, when she saw my age. "You two should really thank your parents." Cindy and I exchanged loaded glances; I could tell that she was trying not to laugh aloud.

"Oh, yeah," she said. "We'll *definitely* do that."

It's true that lurking somewhere in the material we received from each of our parents is the explanation for our similar looks, our shared curiosity and stubbornness, our catalog of similar facial expressions (never more alike than when we are annoyed or skeptical), my impatience, my sister's gentleness. As different as we are—I sometimes feel that every single weakness of mine is somehow magically balanced out, almost neutralized, by her many strengths—the older we get, the more time we spend together, the more I see how we are alike.

Some might say I shouldn't grieve for the years we missed, for how can you miss something, someone, you've never known? Yet I still feel it, all the time, especially as I watch my own two daughters

chatter and play and grow up together. People are always comment-
ing on how similar they look. Even when they annoy each other,
the connection they share is astonishing to me; it's just as deep, as
constant and visceral, as their love for my husband and me, and will
hopefully endure long after we are gone. They were made to go the
distance together, I think; I cannot imagine one of them without the
other.

Cindy and I are recognized as sisters, too, even when we don't
volunteer the information. Our children have mistaken us for one
another, from the back. Every time anyone comments on our similarities, it makes me smile, though I know most of the people looking at us probably imagine we had a shared childhood, like most
other pairs of sisters. It's happened at restaurants, at stores, at the
nail salon: *You're sisters, right? I can just tell.* I like to imagine
that people can tell from the connection between us, the one that
has grown up over the years since we first met—the one that even
a childhood spent apart couldn't fully sever. In my more fanciful
moments, I wonder if others can see my esteem for her, that half
idolizing, almost palpable love I imagine a lot of younger sisters feel.
Maybe people can tell that we, too, belong together, like my own
daughters do. That we, too, were made to go the distance; that we
have always shared a bond, and it was only waiting for us to meet
and make something new.

The last time my older daughter asked me about adoption, I was
honest about the fact that growing up adopted, the only Korean I
knew, was hard for me. She knows that reunion changed everything,
but that it was difficult, too. It was my choice, I have explained to
her; I *wanted* my life to change. I searched because I wasn't content
with what I'd always known—I knew there was more out there.
Reunion has taught me that there is no way to remake your history
or your family in the image you want. But there can be more, if you
are willing to look for those stories that were lost—you might just
find someone new to forgive, to love, to grow with. Someone to take
your hand and search *with* you.

When I went looking for my past, I told my daughter, I had to take what I found, the good and the bad. I would do it all again, a hundred times over, to find my sister. As a sister, I think she understood.

In the end, I think no one was more surprised than my adoptive parents that the story they told me as a child—one they had faithfully passed on to me, despite the holes, the speculation, because they believed in it—bore little resemblance to the truth. While my reunion hasn't always been easy for them, they were genuinely happy when I met Cindy, and have now met her and Rick and my niece Carrie, too. The only thing they all have in common is their love for me, and it turns out that is enough to begin building a friendly relationship.

Since my reunion, my parents have begun to question some of the long-held assumptions about my adoption and the circumstances that led to it. A few months after I met my birth father, my mother asked me, "What do you think about your adoption now? Do you think it was a good thing?" The question represented a possibility we had never before acknowledged. That she might be willing to reconsider the sacred scripture of my childhood—adoption as not just "a good thing," but ordered by God himself—was so shocking I didn't know what to say.

I know my place in my adoptive family is secure. That is not the same thing as always feeling that I belong. My grandmother and my mother will talk about other people in the family, the cousins I do not resemble even slightly—*He looks exactly like John at that age* or *She's Margaret all over*—and I'll know that when they look at me, they can't see generations of people they've known and loved. At some age I cannot identify with certainty, I began to realize that they all felt comfortable, *settled* within our family in ways I still do not at times. It wasn't just our obvious physical differences that made me question if I belonged: when I heard a beloved relative use an Asian slur, refer to a Chinese dish as "flied lice," or joke about not being able to tell Asian people apart—when they would rail about immigration or ask me what I thought about "open borders" or "anchor babies"—when I grew up and we began to argue about our votes and our values—the words *it's because I'm Asian and none of you can understand what it's like* would often be on the edge of my tongue.

Though I've sometimes grieved for absent solidarity, now that I am raising children of color in a starkly divided America I feel, even more strongly, that maintaining my silence with my relatives—pretending my race does not matter—is no longer a choice I can make. It feels like my duty as my white family's de facto Asian ambassador to remind them that I am *not* white, that we *do* experience this country in different ways because of it, that many people still know oppression far more insidious and harmful than anything I've ever faced. Every time I do this, I am breaching the sacred pact of our family, our once-shared belief that my race is irrelevant in the presence of their love. But withholding hard truths and my honest opinions would also sell short the love I have for them, and they for me. The fierce wish I still harbor for them to understand me for who I am, stand with me in love and full acceptance, persists because they chose me and they raised me: we are one another's responsibility.

When my mother asked if I thought my transracial adoption was "a good thing," I was reminded, again, of the fact that I no longer think of it in terms of *good* or *bad*, but *realistic* versus *oversimpli-*

fied. Yes, I often felt alone, unseen in my white family. At times, I still do. But to be adopted is to know only the rewritten story, one of an infinite number possible. I will never be able to honestly say I would have fared better with my birth parents, or any other unknown family.

"I do wish you and Dad had tried to find out more about my birth family," I said. "I could have learned more if I'd just had help."

Now I was within a breath of my birth mother's onetime attempt at contact. I suspected my parents were trying to protect me by "losing" the letter; ensuring I could never read or act on it, even when I was older. But I also knew they were protecting themselves. The terror of having me taken away had never entirely left them— and maybe that was a motivation I would never fully understand, because I had never been in their position.

Sometimes I still wonder what might have happened if they had given my birth mother a different answer. I might have grown up knowing my birth family—knowing their names, at least; knowing their faces. I might have reached an understanding of myself as a Korean, found a way to embrace that fact without shame, many years earlier. I don't know if I would have learned the whole truth, or if it would have been somehow kept from me until Cindy or Jessica could break the rule of family silence and let me in. Still, I might have learned so much more about them. If there were risks, perhaps there would have been certain unexpected gifts as well.

For all my wondering and questions as a child, it's taken me a long time to understand that, as adopters and adoptee, my parents and I will always view my adoption in vastly different ways. *There are some things your parents are never going to fully understand, just because they have never experienced being adopted*, a fellow adoptee told me years ago, before I decided to search for my birth family. The questions that sometimes kept me awake at night, the ones I hoarded and kept to myself, afraid to even scribble in my diary, did not haunt my mother and father at all. It took me many years to recognize and give voice to this fundamental dissonance: their gain was mine, too, but only after I experienced a deep loss. I suspect they are probably a little relieved that I did not find a happy, intact biological family to rejoin.

"We weren't even sure what questions to ask when she reached out through the lawyer," Mom admitted. "The idea of sharing you with them scared us. We never wanted or planned to be in contact with your birth family, and we didn't know how to support you in a more open adoption."

In other words, we were a family, sufficient unto ourselves. My unknown, unseen birth mother had been trying to step out of the shadows—of course my parents had been afraid. I knew this already, but was glad my mother felt able to say it aloud. And when I told her, "Being adopted probably saved my life," it wasn't an appeasement, a melodramatic or magnanimous offering. Reunion had given me many truths, some of them difficult to bear. This was one I would always believe.

They thought adoption was the best thing for you.

They were right, Mom.

"Maybe it would have been good if they had gotten counseling as a family before the adoption," my mother ventured. "Maybe you would have been better off if your birth father had divorced your birth mother earlier, and kept you and Cindy. Then you wouldn't have been separated."

I shook my head a little, not disagreeing so much as acknowledging the impossibility of ever knowing: it was so hard to say, three decades later, what would have been best for the largest number of people. I thought of something Jessica had told me once, when I asked if she ever resented my sudden reappearance and the unearthing of family secrets. *I never blamed you,* she insisted. *I'm glad you opened everything up and showed us the truth. It was hard, but it's the end result that matters.* Remembering her words now, I could better appreciate that wisdom. Maybe I would have been happy growing up with my sister after our parents divorced. And maybe my adoptive parents would have eventually found another child to adopt, one who would have been less of a mystery to them.

But just as I bristled when people clung to platitudes about adoption giving kids "a better life," I was unsure what "better off" would have meant in my own case. Could my birth father have made different choices and raised Cindy and me, together? Of course, but he didn't. He had—like my adoptive parents—done the best he could, improvising a new plan when the first went awry. Even now that we've met, now that I genuinely care for and respect him as the real person he is and not the nebulous, idealized parent I'd once imagined, I find it difficult to imagine growing up as my birth father's child. I don't know if I ever would have measured up to his standards; a part of me will always feel a little relieved I never had to try.

As for my birth mother, we remain estranged, if that is the correct term for a relationship that never truly began. I pity her, for many reasons, though I am certain she wouldn't want me to. Jessica once told me that if our mother had gotten help, if she had been able to go to therapy, she might be different, but there were real barriers: there was no way to pay for the help she likely needed, and even if they'd had the means, she would have had to find a doctor who spoke Korean. When my birth parents were considering adoption for me, the child welfare system that took charge of my placement overlooked the opportunity to look closer and see children at risk, a family in crisis.

When she called out of the blue one Saturday not long ago, as I stood on the sidelines at my daughter's soccer game, I answered and then froze when I realized who it was—much like I had all those years ago when Abby was just one week old. I thought, *Here's where you ask her not to call again.* But I didn't. I've squandered so many chances to tell her I don't want to talk to her again. I'm incapable of imagining her in my life, and apparently also incapable of telling her to forget about me. Sometimes I can't do it because her sins, while real, are not against me. Sometimes I don't because I don't want to give her one more thing to hold against Cindy. Sometimes I think about how she tried to find me when I was little, only to be turned away like a beggar at the gates.

And I know that if I told her, *I know who you are and that's why I don't want anything to do with you*, it would be false—her actions have ensured I'll *never* truly know who she is. It is a different kind of ache than the pain of abandonment I once knew, the self-doubts and sense of inadequacy with which I grew up. It still hurts, but it's a hurt I can understand, a sorrow I can bear, because I now know the reasons for it.

"I hope that now there is more knowledge and compassion in adoption," my mother said to me not long after my reunion, "so that more birth parents and adoptive parents can figure out what's best for them and their kids."

I nodded, *of course*; it was like something plucked from my own head, a line I might offer to those considering adoption. Only later did it occur to me that this and other discussions with my mother would have seemed impossible before I found my birth family.

Until I decided to search, my adoption, important as it was, remained a single, settled matter relegated to the past—none of us had any reason to reconsider it. Reunion has done more than restore relationships that had once been beyond my ability to fully imagine; it has enabled a shift in existing ones. It has forced my adoptive parents to think about my birth parents not as poor, pitiable immigrants or people who might steal me away, but real people with their own feelings, fears, and failings. It's forced them to think about how I must have felt when I lost not only my first family, but all knowledge of my roots.

I won't ever regret my search or my reunion; how both opened up new possibilities while closing others. I am thankful to know my birth father, even just a little; to have met Cindy and talked with Jessica. My birth family's importance, their place in my life, can never be denied again. But one thing has not wavered or changed: I am still my adoptive parents' daughter. No matter what, no matter our differences, they will always be my parents, the ones who wanted me when no one else did.

Mama, am I a real Korean?"

Abby was five years and a few days old, perched on the edge of our couch, one finger hooked around the edge of her book. She asked me questions all the time, and had been doing so ever since she began to talk, but somehow I had never imagined her asking this one—why? Before I could recover, or reach for an answer, she added, "Because I don't think I am."

I watched the furrow on her brow deepen. This was a moment, brand-new, that somehow felt so familiar; it was one I'd always feared for her, and hoped she could somehow avoid. "What do you mean, honey?"

"I don't know how to speak Korean," she said. "I think that means I must not be a real one."

I closed my eyes briefly. She didn't seem upset, just puzzled—but I couldn't help but feel upset on her behalf. Why had I been unprepared for this moment? How many times had I said the exact same thing to myself?

She went on to tell me that her "real" Chinese friends at school spoke Chinese, and one of them had asked her if she was

Chinese, too. "I told her that you were Korean, and that I was Korean and Irish and Lemonese."

"Lebanese."

"Lebanese. And then she asked if I could speak Korean. I said I couldn't, and she said, 'Then how do you know you're really Korean?'"

As an adoptee, I was well aware that my multiracial kids would one day have far more difficult, more complex questions of identity to answer for themselves—questions that could not be answered with a language litmus test. Abby had already overheard comments from strangers curious about her and her sister—*So, what are they, exactly?*—and she knew that our family looked different from some other families, not just because I was adopted. For the time being, though, while I could still provide some answers, I just wanted to reassure my older daughter. Wasn't that why I had sought out my birth family in the first place—so that she wouldn't have to doubt who she was, wonder about her history, the way I always had?

"You *are* a real Korean," I said. "Lots of Koreans who live in America can't speak the language, or don't speak it well."

"Auntie Cindy speaks Korean," she pointed out. I smiled again: I would always feel happy when reminded of the wondrous fact that my children had always known Cindy as their aunt, had spent vacations and holidays with her family, and adored her and their uncle and little cousin. "Does Carrie speak Korean?" she added, referring to Cindy and Rick's daughter, born two months before Grace.

"Carrie is little. Cindy might have taught her a little Korean, but not much."

"*I* want to learn Korean. You should learn how to talk in Korean first, and then you can teach me."

"Sweetheart," I said, laughing in spite of the twinge in my heart, "it takes a long time to learn a language. Even if I started right now, I'm not sure when I would know enough to be able to teach you."

Looking at my bewildered child, I was suddenly reminded of the time she had asked me how airplanes stayed up in the air. I told her I would need to look it up to be able to fully understand and explain it to her, and she exclaimed, almost scandalized, "But you're a grown-up! You've had your whole *life* to learn everything!" I had explained to her that even the smartest grown-up couldn't possibly learn everything there was to know in the world. Her answering expression, one of mingled shock and deep disappointment, rooted itself in my memory. She wore the exact same look now as she watched me hedge on Korean lessons.

I *had* thought about trying to study Korean, though I had yet to pursue it between having her little sister and beginning graduate school. Studying a language was only one of many ways to feel connected to a culture, a history, a clan, but to me it had always seemed an important one. In college I had briefly considered enrolling in a Korean course, until I realized most of the other students were Koreans looking to "brush up"—I could not imagine anything that would make me feel like more of an imposter than starting from scratch in a room of near-fluent speakers. I had always envied other Koreans I knew who spoke the language so effortlessly, including my birth father and my sister; their cultural identities had seemed infinitely more natural, less ambiguous than my own.

Now I felt the same heavy inadequacy I had experienced when I was pregnant with Abby. I hadn't been able to bear the thought of her growing up without her history; I had focused on reconnecting with my birth family, restoring those ties, believing that both she and I would benefit from it. And we had. I knew I would never stop feeling awed by this child who had inspired me, months before she was even born, to search for my birth family and my lost roots.

But currently her only understanding of her identity seemed to stem from the knowledge that she was not just one race or the other, and I wasn't sure how to help her understand or feel proud of her mixed heritage, in all its fullness and complexity. I didn't want her to always define herself in terms of the negative: *I'm not this* or *that*. I wanted her to be able to say—as I had not—*This is who I am.*

I thought about the words of a fellow adoptee and mother of a little girl, shared with me not long after I became a parent. "Being able to have a child, this biological connection, has meant everything to me," she'd told me. "Everything she does, I'm amazed. I'm going to give her everything I can, teach her everything I can, share with her everything I can." Perhaps studying a little Korean would be a fun and logical way to start filling in the gaps for my curious daughter. And what else might I do? I could try out my sister's recipes, ones I had watched her prepare for us during visits. I could take out the *hanbok* my birth father and his wife had bought for our family in Korea and maybe even wear them sometime. Someday—we talked about it often—Cindy and I planned to take our children to Korea, so she could show all of us around together. I still hoped we might be able to do this before all our relatives there were gone.

I tried to ignore the voice of doubt suggesting that perhaps I had no right to any of this; that all of it, country visit and potential language study included, represented little more than a glorified, grasping form of cultural appropriation. If not for the adoption, I wouldn't have thought twice about these things being part of my birthright. I had gained so much since I set out to find my birth family: another family, a deeper understanding of my history and my identity, people with whom I knew that I belonged. I had found Cindy, beyond any hope or expectation I had ever entertained in my wildest childhood imaginings. If *that* were possible—if a stranger could become my sister—surely I could also find some way to regain at least some part of my heritage, my cultural birthright, and pass on that knowledge and sense of belonging to my daughters.

"I'll see what I can do," I told Abby, and watched her break into a grin. "It's going to be hard work, you know."

"I can work very hard, Mama. And I hope you learn really fast so you can teach me," she said. "But it's fine if it takes a month or two. There are a lot of other things I have to focus on, like getting better on my bike."

I found several local Korean schools affiliated with churches, but no one returned my calls—except for one man who informed me that the Korean school was for children (and native speakers) only. "Are you a child?" he demanded. When I admitted I was not, he hung up on me. Finally, after weeks of searching and calling around, a private tutor named Angie responded. I couldn't help but think of a Korean American friend with the same name, who'd been a kind of big sister to me in college, years before I found my birth family. *Nicole, I received your message about wanting to learn Korean. I would be happy to teach you. How is this Friday evening for you?*

We arranged to meet at a coffee shop in the sprawling shopping complex down the road from my house. A woman I guessed to be in her forties, shorter and slimmer than me, Angie easily identified me near the pastry case. We found a table in the back of the coffee shop. She chuckled as she inspected me from behind rimless rectangular glasses. "When you told me that you had two children, I was expecting someone a lot older," she said, over the low chatter of evening customers and the click of laptop keys one table over. "Why do you want to learn Korean?"

When I explained that I was adopted, and had not grown up speaking the language, her eyebrows disappeared under neat black bangs. "Your adoptive parents couldn't find someone to teach you?" At this I was a bit taken aback; I had heard of adoptees of younger generations taking language lessons, learning to cook certain dishes, studying cultural dance or music, thanks to the newer focus on adoptive families celebrating a child's heritage, but there had been few opportunities like that when I was a child. I doubted it had ever occurred to my adoptive parents that I might *want* to learn anything about Korea. Had they ever suggested a language class, I'm sure I would have complained—it was bad enough that I couldn't change the way I looked; did I really have to emphasize my differences by learning a language no one else I knew could speak?

Angie produced a colorful workbook from her bag and pushed it across the table toward me. Smiling children—none of whom appeared to be Korean—danced in a circle around the book's pale yellow cover. The cover wear and faint pencil markings along the edges made it clear that the book wasn't new. It was a children's book, of course, because I knew less than a child.

"This book used to be my son's," she said, opening to a page filled with characters that I recognized as consonants. "When he was young I tried to teach him Korean, but he never wanted to study. He's just like you now—you know, very Americanized."

Over the next hour, as my oversweetened black tea grew cold, Angie took me through all of the Korean consonants and vowels one by one. I did my best to parrot her pronunciations and write each character on a piece of scratch paper. Then we began pairing them up so that I could see how syllables and words were constructed. When she told me, "You know, you kind of say the words like a native speaker," I felt absurdly pleased with myself, like a child praised by her schoolteacher.

I committed most of the new letters to mind right there at the table, thanks to a strong visual memory; I found I could copy them with surprising speed. They were easier than the Japanese character sets I'd learned in high school. Letters bloomed from my pencil, diminutive bars and circles and boxes that I would have to learn to decode. "You see how easy it is to write in Korean," Angie said. "Now that you know these, you can put them together to make words. What do you want to write? Did your parents give you a Korean name?"

At her urging, I carefully wrote my Korean name on a fresh piece of paper, the name my birth father had chosen for me. In English, he spelled my first name *Soo Jung*, but in Korean its second syllable was actually identical to the family name: 정, Romanized as *Chung* in our family and pronounced more like *Jung*. 정수정, my full Korean birth name rendered in my new, shaky Hangul. For fun, I also wrote Cindy's name: 정인정. I loved seeing our names, our common syllables, side by side: they had long bound us together without our knowledge, even though we had grown up apart.

Angie showed me the page in the book on introductions. She wrote and then read the line for me to parrot back, using my Korean name. "'*Je ireumeun Jung Soo Jung imnida*.'"

It wasn't, though it had been once. I hesitated, wondering if I should change the phrase, use my actual name. Instead I took a deep breath and repeated the words, trying to own and internalize the everyday statement that felt, to me, extraordinary.

She had me say it again, and again, making tiny adjustments to my pronunciation, and each time my voice got a little stronger. I had never claimed my birth name, associated myself or introduced myself with it, in English. It was strange to do so even in Korean, for an audience of one, but I felt like less of an imposter than I expected to. It made me wonder if there might come a day when I would reclaim my birth name, in part or in its entirety, as some other adopted people I knew had done.

By the time Angie concluded our lesson, an employee was sweeping up nearby, circling closer as we stood up to leave. I looked around, surprised to realize how much time had passed; we were the last customers in the café. "I want you to master the alphabet for next time," the tutor said, handing me her son's old book. "You should be able to write all the letters, and combine them into words, without looking at the book."

I agreed with considerably more confidence than I felt. Yet I did feel heartened, even excited, as I slid the workbook into my bag. She hadn't laughed at me, accused me of not being a "real" Korean, or told me it was impossible to learn at my age. While vowels and consonants were only the building blocks of words and sentences, the letters that filled my paper in neat, orderly columns already looked familiar—like new acquaintances, if not old friends. This language, the language of my original family, seemed just a little less mysterious than it had before.

Abby discovered my workbook on the dining room table the following morning, and wasted no time in commandeering it. As I made myself breakfast in the kitchen, I heard her firing questions at Dan, who had no way of answering. "What does this say? What is this word here? How do I write my name in Korean?"

She worked diligently at her little desk in the living room while I ate my eggs and toast. By the time I finished my coffee, she was ready to show me her results. "Mama," she said, thrusting a piece of yellow construction paper into my hands, "look what I just did!"

She had written all of the Korean consonants, followed by all the vowels, and labeled them with their corresponding sounds. There were a few cross-outs, a few tiny errors, but I had no trouble discerning each character. Though I wasn't at all surprised by her enthusiasm, her effort impressed me. I asked if she wanted to help me practice my letters, too. Working side by side, Angie's workbook lying open on the table between us, we picked out words to write. Family. *Gajok.* Tree. *Namu.* Story. *Iyagi.* Abby drew a small picture of a butterfly next to the word *nabi.*

Not long after we met, Cindy had informed me with unmistakable fondness that everything about me "screams 'American.'" I knew I could spend the rest of my life seeking, and still regain only a fraction of what I had lost. But as I looked over my child's first attempt at writing in Korean, I felt sure that I had made the right decision to search. Introducing her first to her aunt, then to her biological grandfather, and now to this first symbol of our shared heritage—these were all aspects of healing, though I hadn't realized I still needed to be healed. My identity as an adoptee is complicated, fluid, but then so is everyone else's.

Again I thought back to Abby's question—*Am I a real Korean?*—an unintentional echo of a question I'd asked myself so many times.

221

From the moment I learned that I was carrying her, I had been startled by all the things parenthood had pushed me into doing, all the questions and doubts it had raised. Just by existing, both my daughters continually made me reflect on who I was and who I wanted to be; the messy family history and shifting Korean and American identities I so badly wanted to understand and help *them* understand.

The adoption story I'd heard so often growing up was supposed to remake me, give me everything I needed, make me feel whole. In the end, though, real growth and healing came from another kind of radical change—from finding the courage to question what I'd always been told; to seek and discover and tell another kind of story. And I know my children will benefit from all the things I will pass on to them now, all the truths I'm able to share.

"What should we write now, Mama?" Abby asked, tapping the workbook with the tip of her pencil. "The alphabet, again?"

I turned back to the first page of our shared book. My eyes scanned the newly familiar characters in their boxes, the rows of letters waiting to be transformed into syllables and sentences and perhaps even new stories for both of us. I nodded at my daughter, meeting her curious look with a smile. "Yes," I said. "Let's start at the beginning."

ACKNOWLEDGMENTS

This story owes its life to my kind and brilliant editor, Julie Buntin, who sent me an email way back in November 2015 to ask if I was working on anything (I was!). Julie fought for this book from day one, banked up my faith at every turn, improved my manuscript at every stage, and didn't even freak out when I told her I was reorganizing the entire first half based on a dream I'd had. How incredible is Julie? She edited huge chunks of this *while on her own book tour.* I will always be grateful to her.

Working on your first book can make you feel like a little kid sneaking into the big kids' amusement park ride. This journey would have been so much more daunting without the steady reassurance, support, and faith of my agent, Maria Massie. Thanks also to Shannon O'Neill, one of the very first people to listen and help me define this story; and to Amanda Annis, erstwhile editor turned agent, advocate, and editorial matchmaker.

Thank you to everyone at Catapult who supported this book beyond my wildest hopes, politely refusing to comment on the fact that for like a year I was too anxious to look any of them in the eye when it came up. No book or author could have better champions than Julie, Andy Hunter, Jennifer Abel Kovitz, Megan Fishmann,

Lena Moses-Schmitt, Erin Kottke, Katie Boland, Sarah Baline, and Dustin Kurtz. Every time I thought I was about to lose my grip, a reassuring email from Jonathan Lee or Pat Strachan would pop up in the nick of time. Donna Cheng and Nicole Caputo came up with a beautiful design for the hardcover edition that made the book 25 percent better, just like that. Thank you to the patient and skilled Jordan Koluch, Wah-Ming Chang, and Elizabeth Ireland; to Colin Drohan and Stella Cabot Wilson, who supported Julie while she worked on this book and fielded all my frantic texts; and to my web editorial colleagues past and present, including Yuka Igarashi, Megha Majumdar, Mensah Demary, Allie Wuest, Mallory Soto, Morgan Jerkins, and Natalie Degraffinried. Special thanks to Yuka, one of the greatest and most gracious mentors I've ever had, for making me part of a wonderful editorial team, advocating for this book, and providing so much crucial input and encouragement during the writing.

My love and gratitude, always, to Nicole Cliffe and Daniel Mallory Ortberg, who know every reason why.

A thousand thanks to friends and early manuscript readers Kat Chow, Angela Chen, Noah Cho, Spencer Lee Lenfield, Matthew Salesses, JaeRan Kim, and Rita Maldonado.

No one should go through their debut alone—I am so grateful for the friendship and surpassingly beautiful books of R. O. Kwon, Ingrid Rojas Contreras, Vanessa Hua, Lydia Kiesling, Crystal Hana Kim, Lillian Li, and Lucy Tan.

Thank you to the friends, writers, and teachers to whom I owe so much, including Taylor Harris, Tope Charlton, Alyssa Keiko Furukawa, Karissa Chen, Celeste Ng, Laura Ortberg Turner, Elon Green, Esmé Weijun Wang, Greg Pak, Alexander Chee, Jaya Saxena, Jess Zimmerman, Min Jin Lee, Rainbow Rowell, Jessica Valenti, Jasmine Guillory, Kendra James, Arissa Oh, Chanda Prescod-Weinstein, Rahawa Haile, Rose Eveleth, Sarah Werner, Kirstin Butler, Kathleen Fitzpatrick, Emily Brooks, Margaret H. Willison, Heather Cocks and Jessica Morgan, Beth Kephart, Tim Wendel, Ralph Burrelle, and Susan Champion.

Cheers to *The Toast* and Toasties everywhere, to *Hyphen* magazine, to Kundiman, and to every editor who's given me a chance.

Whenever I was afraid working on this book (and there were many, many times when that was the case), thinking of my fellow adoptees is what kept me going. Thank you to every adopted person reading this. And to every adoptee I've ever read, learned from, or published—I can't imagine where or who I would be without your voices.

Finally, this memoir would not exist without the love and patience of my many families. Thank you, Dan, for making our life not just possible, but wonderful, and for working harder than anyone else to support my dreams. Thank you, Cindy, for being the family I didn't know or dare to hope for, and for saying yes when I asked if I could write about it all. Thank you to my mom for raising me with love, and for reading this book and seeing only more love and truth; and to my birth father and his wife and Rick and Jessica for every story shared and every door so generously opened to me. Thanks to Marie, John, Meghan, Tom, and Abra for all the support and sustenance over the years. Dad, I miss you every day, but I know you're still proud of me—I'm glad your joke stayed in, too.

And to the nineteenth generation—the *best* generation, as far as I'm concerned—this story is yours, too. I hope you like it. You are loved.